W9-ADN-761

CATHOLICS IN WESTERN DEMOCRACIES

Other books by the same author:
Church and State in Modern Ireland 1923-79
(second edition, 1980)
The Independent Irish Party, 1850–9 (1958)

JOHN H. WHYTE

CATHOLICS IN WESTERN DEMOCRACIES

A STUDY IN POLITICAL BEHAVIOUR

GILL AND MACMILLAN

First published 1981 by
Gill and Macmillan Ltd
Goldenbridge
Dublin 8
with associated companies in
London, New York, Delhi, Hong Kong,
Johannesburg, Lagos, Melbourne,
Singapore, Tokyo

7171 1129 6

Origination by Computertype Limited, Dublin

Printed in Great Britain by
Photobooks (Bristol) Limited

Contents

List of Tables

Introduction

I can best explain the purpose of this book by a word of autobiography. For over twenty years, from the time that I first registered as a graduate student in 1949, until I published a book called *Church and State in Modern Ireland* in 1971, most of my research was concerned in one way or another with the political behaviour of Irish Roman Catholics. Working as a historian in the nineteen-fifties, I studied various aspects of nineteenth-century Irish politics, in which the role of the Church inevitably loomed large. As a political scientist in the nineteen-sixties, I studied the role of the Church in twentieth-century Ireland. During those years, questions which constantly teased me were – How far was the situation I was examining typical of Catholicism as a whole? Did Catholics in other countries behave in similar ways in such circumstances? If not, how did they behave? Was there such a thing as a 'normal' political pattern for Catholics, from which Irish Catholics did or did not diverge? I read very widely in the history of Catholicism in other countries, hoping to find answers to such questions. I never found a book which gave me quite what I needed. In the end I decided that, if I wanted such a book, I would have to write it myself. The present work is the result.

However, I have not written it just to indulge a private curiosity. My hope is that it will interest other people besides myself. I have three potential audiences in mind. First, there are people studying the political behaviour of Catholics in particular countries. I am sure that some of them must have felt, as I have, the lack of a general theory of the political behaviour of Catholics against which to measure their findings. I hope that this book may be a first step towards meeting their needs. Such people should amount to a considerable number, for Catholicism impinges or has impinged on the politics of a remarkable number of countries. Nearly all the countries of Europe, North and South America, Australia and to a lesser extent New Zealand, several countries in Asia and a number in Africa: all told, the number of countries where there is or has been a 'Catholic factor' in politics totals more than eighty of the world's hundred and sixty states.

Second, there are political scientists with an interest in the comparative study of political cleavages. This has been a growth area of political science over the last twenty-five years. Scholars such as Lipset, Rokkan, Alford, Rose, Urwin and Lijphart have examined, with increasing sophistication, the interconnections between class, religion, language and other factors underpinning the political divisions of different countries. One conclusion to emerge from their work has been the continuing importance of religion as a basis for political cleavage. Among religions, Catholicism ranks one of the highest in its ability to generate both loyalty and hostility. A study of the political behaviour of Catholics should, then, contribute considerably to the wider study of political cleavages.

Third, there are sociologists with a special interest in religion. Since the time of Weber and Durkheim, such scholars have formed an important group within the discipline of sociology. Weber sparked off a discussion of the comparative effects of Catholicism and Protestantism which has continued to the present day. Many scholars, particularly in America, have offered triple comparisons of Protestants, Catholics and Jews. Some have compared the effects of Christianity and eastern religions. Yet others have examined the differences between varieties of Protestantism or of Islam. One topic which has been surprisingly neglected is that of variations within catholicism. Anyone who has had experience of catholicism in a number of different countries will know that it can vary greatly in ethos and effects. This is a field wide open to systematic scholarly study. Almost the only sociologist to have entered it so far was the late Ivan Vallier. He produced a stimulating typology of Catholicisms, based on his findings in Latin America. I shall discuss the parallels between his conclusions and my own in Appendix A. There remains a great deal to be done; as a political scientist, I can explore only one corner of this field. Perhaps sociologists, with a concern for a wider range of institutions, will find some interest in what I have to say, and will ask whether the patterns which seem to prevail in politics are also applicable to other fields of activity.

The decision to write such a book as this required a decision on a number of other points. What should be the geographical coverage: world-wide or confined to one group or type of countries? Ideally, coverage should be world-wide, encompassing dictatorships and democracies, rich and poor states. Only in that way could one be sure that conclusions are not distorted by the absence of some significant group of countries. However, in this pioneer study, I decided to confine myself to western democracies. The practical argument for restricting my scope proved overwhelming. It has taken me several years' work to produce even the present study. To have extended it to the whole world would have at least trebled the amount of work. Furthermore, in a book which originated in an attempt to put Ireland in a comparative context, it seemed reasonable to concentrate on democratic states. However, if the present work arouses any interest, I would hope to amplify and if need be correct its findings in a more comprehensive study.

The category of western democracies is one widely used by political scientists, and there is a large measure of agreement on what countries qualify for inclusion. The criteria appear to be: (a) that the country have a continuous history of working democratic institutions going back at least to the end of the Second World War (a criterion which excludes Spain and Portugal); (b) that it be economically advanced; and (c) that it be European in geographical location or at least in cultural origin. In five different authorities, I found the range of countries included in the category varying only between nineteen and twenty-three. Nineteen countries were listed by all five authorities, one (Israel) by four, and no other country by more than two.[1] If I take the nineteen countries listed by all five authorities as my starting point, I can at once exclude the five Nordic states from further consideration in this book because their Catholic populations are negligible. I have had to exclude Luxembourg also, because I was unable to find sufficient data on it. This leaves me with a universe of thirteen countries which are unquestionably western democracies and have a Catholic population large enough to be politically significant. These thirteen countries will be singled out for study in this book:

Australia	Austria	Belgium	Canada
France	Germany	Ireland	Italy
The Netherlands	New Zealand	Switzerland	United Kingdom
United States			

One problem resulting from this choice of countries may be mentioned here: some of them do not have a continuous history within their present frontiers. The United Kingdom and Ireland were the same state until 1921. Canada and Australia were formed by federating previously distinct colonies, in 1867–73 and 1900 respectively. Canada did not absorb Newfoundland until 1949. The present Federal Republic of Germany contains only a little over half the area of the inter-war Weimar Republic; that in its turn was smaller than the German Empire of 1871–1918. Austria has undergone even more dramatic changes. Before 1918, it was part of a huge multi-national empire, Austria-Hungary. I have been able to ignore the Hungarian component because, although it joined with Austria for international affairs, its internal politics were distinct. But even the non-Hungarian part of the empire – what was sometimes called Cisleithanian Austria – was much larger and more diverse than the present-day Austrian republic. It included territories which have since gone to Poland, Czechoslovakia, Yugoslavia and Italy. However, since they all sent representatives to the same parliament, there was no way of including the present Austria while excluding the rest. Readers must bear in mind, then, that in this book 'German' does not mean the same thing before 1918 or before 1933 as it does after 1945; and that 'Austria' covers a radically different area before 1918 than subsequently.

A second decision to be taken was: what sort of Catholic

should I study? In this book, 'Catholic' and 'Catholicism' are shorthand for 'Roman Catholic' and 'Roman Catholicism', but that leaves a great deal unanswered. For Catholics are not all of a piece. They vary in their commitment from the most fervent to the most nominal. To attempt to include nominal Catholics in the analysis could produce considerably different results from including only the fervent. To take one example out of many, in France and Italy many nominal Catholics vote Communist, but hardly any fervent ones do. At what point, then, can one best make the cut-off between those Catholics who are worth studying *as Catholics,* and those whose adherence to the Church is so loose as to exercise little influence on their political behaviour? Fortunately, the canon law of the Church provides a criterion by which the committed can be distinguished from the indifferent. It lays down that every Catholic over the age of seven should, unless prevented by good reason, attend mass every weekend. (Canon law also imposes other obligations, but they can be left aside in the present context.) A Catholic who tries to get to mass every weekend is normally called a 'practising Catholic'; one who does not is described as 'non-practising'. Weekly mass-goers may not be any more moral than their non-churchgoing fellow-Catholics; but the fact that they fulfil the obligation imposed by canon law shows that they are concerned to maintain their link with the institutional Church. One might expect, then, that the institutional Church would shape their outlook to an extent that does not apply to non-practising Catholics.

This supposition is borne out by research in a number of countries. In mixed Protestant-Catholic countries such as Germany, the Netherlands and Switzerland, surveys indicate that, while Catholics as a whole have different voting patterns from Protestants as a whole, the differences between practising and non-practising Catholics are even sharper.[2] Particularly interesting evidence comes from a careful analysis by Michelat and Simon of survey data from France collected in 1966. They distinguished four categories among their respondents: practising Catholics (attending church once a week or more); irregularly practising Catholics (attending church several times a year); non-practising

Catholics; and those with no religion. They found that the difference between the first group and the other three was particularly significant:

> The higher the level of religious integration, the tighter the link between political behaviour and the religious variable. Once one passes the threshold of regular religious practice, voting and political attitudes almost cease to depend on any other variable, and we have been unable to find any common characteristic other than the religious one to explain the very strong political homogeneity of practising Catholics. On the other hand, as the level of religious integration is lowered, political behaviour is increasingly influenced by other variables, particularly objective and subjective social class.

And again:

> Workers who are children of workers rarely practise. But when they do, their political behaviour – and, it would seem, the values which underlie that behaviour – are scarcely distinguishable from those of people with the same level of practice who have no working-class background.[3]

In other words, for the practising Catholic, religion was the crucial determinant of political behaviour, while for Catholics whose attachment to the Church was loose or nominal, other factors mattered more.

I shall, therefore, in this book concentrate on the behaviour of *practising* Catholics, i.e. of those who take seriously their obligation to attend mass weekly. This will not always be easy because, particularly before survey evidence became plentiful, the sources often do not clearly state what kind of Catholic they are discussing. It can be taken that, whenever I refer *tout court* to 'Catholics', I mean 'practising Catholics', or least 'practising Catholics in so far as their political behaviour can be distinguished', unless I specifically state otherwise.

A third decision that had to be taken was: how best to order the material. For the variety of political behaviour displayed by Catholics – even if we confine ourselves to western democracies – has been bewildering. In some countries, Catholics have been virtually united behind a single political party. In others, they have had no party of their own, but have divided between non-denominational parties in much the same proportions as other citizens. In some countries, they have built up separate Catholic trade unions, farmers' associations, youth movements, and social organisations of all kinds. In others, they have participated in the same social organisations as the rest of the population. In some, bishops have issued a stream of directives to the faithful on how they should vote at elections; in others, they have remained silent. In some, priests have served as members of parliament and cabinet ministers; in others, they have played no part in politics. In some countries, the clergy have been much divided politically, between secular priests and members of religious orders, or between bishops and lower clergy, or between priests of different nationalities; in others, they have been relatively united. The role played by the papacy has varied: it has taken a more direct interest in the politics of some countries – Italy most notably, but also France – than of others. Catholics have also differed in their position on the left-right spectrum: in some countries they have been a more conservative force than in others. All these factors vary, not just between countries, but between different periods in the history of the same country.

In a pioneering study such as this one, it is not possible to take account of all the variations just listed. It has proved possible, however, to find some unifying principle for the majority of them. I have done this by applying a well-known device in the social sciences, the formulation of 'ideal types'. Most of the varieties of Catholic behaviour listed in the preceding paragraph can be placed somewhere on a spectrum whose end-points are defined by two ideal types which I shall describe as closed and open Catholicism.

The characteristics of *closed Catholicism* are as follows:

1. A Catholic political party exists which receives the support of all Catholics and no non-Catholics.
2. The Catholic party is linked to Catholic social organisations. Trade unions, farmers', employers', youth and welfare organisations, and so on are run on a confessional basis: Catholics join exclusively Catholic organisations.
3. The Catholic population is under strong clerical guidance.

At election times, the clergy tell the people that it is their moral duty to vote for the Catholic party and will refuse the sacraments to those who disobey. Clergy take the lead in running the Catholic party and social organisations.

The characteristics of *open Catholicism* are the opposite:

1. There is no Catholic party, nor even any party which receives a disproportionate amount of Catholic support. Where a multi-party system exists, Catholics divide their support between parties in the same proportions as the rest of the population. Where one party dominates, Catholics are neither more nor less prominent in the single party than the population as a whole.
2. Social organisations are organised on a non-confessional basis. Catholics participate in such organisations to the same degree as the rest of the population.
3. The clergy play no part in politics. They neither give advice, nor share in the running of parties or social organisations.

As is usual with the ideal types invented by social scientists, neither of these exists in a pure form anywhere in the real world. Even in a country like Britain, where there are no Catholic parties and only feeble Catholic social organisations and where the clergy have generally been cautious about political involvement, Cardinal Heenan could still give a warning in the general election of February 1974 against voting for Communist candidates. Even in a country like the Netherlands between the wars, in which the Catholic party was led by a priest and the mobilisation of Catholics in their parties and social organisations was almost total, it was still possible for dissident Catholics to launch splinter parties and win a few votes. Most countries fall somewhere in between the two ends of the spectrum. A common phenomenon, for instance, is that no specific Catholic party exists, but that Catholics do tend to support one party more than another – as in Germany, where they are more likely to vote Christian Democrat than Social Democrat, or the United States, where they are more likely to vote Democrat than Republican. Nevertheless, the employment of these ideal types does help us to classify differences in Catholic political behaviour. We can describe Catholics in, say, Belgium as falling nearer to the closed end of the spectrum than Catholics in, say, Australia. And we can say that Catholics in Belgium were nearer to the closed end of the spectrum twenty years ago than they are today.

An objection to the use of these ideal types is that the three elements of which they are composed are logically distinct and need not fluctuate in unison. Catholic parties are not always at their strongest at the same time and place as Catholic social organisations. Italy had active Catholic social organisations before it had a Catholic political party. On the other hand, Germany had a strong Catholic political party (the Centre party) when Catholic social organisations were still in their infancy. More important, the political involvement of the clergy has not always varied with the other elements in closed Catholicism. In France, the period of maximum activity by the clergy – the late nineteenth and early twentieth centuries – preceded by several decades the period when parties and social organisations of Catholic inspiration were at their strongest. On the other hand, Catholic parties and social organisations acquire a momentum of their own and many continue vigorous long after the clergy have withdrawn from any active role in them: an example would be the People's party in Austria. None the less, I have found that in practice the three elements move roughly in parallel, and that it is possible to treat them together in a single analysis.

There is one aspect of Catholic political behaviour which I should like to consider, but which I have not found possible to fit into the closed-open typology. This is the position of Catholics on the right-left axis. There is an initial pitfall here: that of deciding what the terms 'right' and 'left' mean. In practice this has not proved too serious a problem: it has generally been clear enough what attitudes were considered 'right-wing' and what 'left-wing' in a given society. But even if the difficulty of definition has been solved, no simple correlation appears between the position of Catholics on the left-right axis and their position on the closed-open one. Open Catholicism in particular can occur in both left-wing and right-wing forms. Yet the two do not vary totally at random: there is some connection between movement of Catholics on the closed-open axis, and movement on the left-right one. I shall devote some space in subsequent chapters to elucidating the relationship between the two.

This book, then, is an attempt to describe and explain the variations in the political behaviour of Catholics along two distinct axes. They can be pictured diagrammatically as follows.

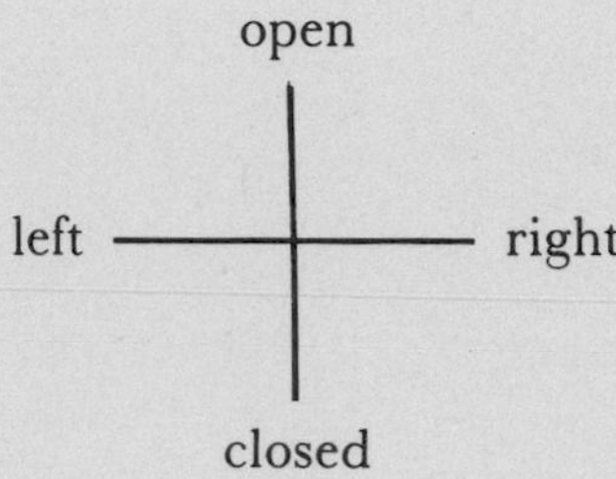

It would make the structure of the book impossibly complicated, however, if both were given equal weight. I shall therefore take the study of the closed-open axis as my main theme, round which the book will be organised. Study of the left-right axis will be a subordinate theme to which reference will be made *en passant,* and generalisations about it will be pulled together in the concluding chapter.

A fourth and final point on which a decision had to be taken was the system of referencing. In a book like this, which is largely derived from standard authorities, I felt that there was no need to document every statement. I have provided a lengthy bibliography, arranged geographically, from which the reader should be able to deduce what sources I have used for particular topics. I have used footnotes only for quotations and for statements which I thought might seem surprising or controversial.

I should like to close by thanking those institutions and individuals who have helped me in the preparation of this work. The Center for International Affairs of Harvard University gave me hospitality in the academic year 1973–4, when I wrote the first draft of this book. The Netherlands Institute for Advanced Study at Wassenaar awarded me a fellowship in the year 1979–80, which provided me with an invaluable opportunity to complete the work, after a period of four years in which I had been diverted into research on another topic. The Queen's University of Belfast twice accorded me leave of absence. The workshops of the European Consortium for Political Research twice provided me with forums in which to try out some of the ideas contained in this book: in London (1975) and Brussels (1979). The text was expertly typed by Ellen Hoff of the Netherlands Institute for Advanced Study and by Pauline McElhill of the Queen's University of Belfast. The following scholars read part or all of the work in draft and provided valuable suggestions: Suzanne Berger, John Bossy, John Coakley, Michael Fogarty, Tom Mackie, Patrick O'Farrell, Cornelius O'Leary, Paul Sacks, Derek Urwin and Henry Valen. The usual disclaimer applies, that none of them is responsible for the shortcomings of this book; but it is perhaps even more valid than usual on this occasion, because the version which most of them saw is considerably different from the one now published. Most important of all, my wife and family provided the environment in which this book could be written.

1

Variations over space

The most obvious way to trace the variations between closed and open Catholicism is territorially. The countries under examination in this book fall into two clearly demarcated groups, the continental European and the Anglo-American:

Continental European		**Anglo-American**	
Austria	Italy	Australia	New Zealand
Belgium	The Netherlands	Canada	United Kingdom
France	Switzerland	Ireland	United States
Germany			

Each group has distinct traditions: the continent of Europe tends towards closed Catholicism, while the Anglo-American countries tend towards open. This is borne out if we examine in turn the three components of the closed-open dichotomy: political parties, social organisations, and clerical activity. Taking parties first, we find that continental Europe is the home of the denominational party. In all countries of the region, parties appealing to Catholic principles and supported preponderantly by Catholics have been for varying periods a major force in politics: the Christian-Social party and then the People's party in Austria; the Catholic party and then the Christian-Social party in Belgium; the *Mouvement républicain populaire* in post-war France; the Centre party in pre-war Germany; the Popular party and later the Christian Democrats in Italy; the Catholic party under various titles in the Netherlands; the Christian Democratic People's party and its forerunners in Switzerland. German Catholics have since 1945 united with many German Protestants in supporting the inter-denominational Christian Democrats, but Catholic influence in that party remains strong. The Dutch Catholic party joined with two Protestant parties in 1976 to form a new grouping, the Christian Democratic Appeal, but its members remain influential in the new party. Only in France has a distinct Christian Democratic party ceased to exist: the Christian Democratic tradition is now represented as a tendency within President Giscard d'Estaing's *Union pour la démocratie française*.

In the Anglo-American countries on the other hand, examples of what could by any stretch of the imagination be called Catholic parties have been rare, often with a limited territorial base. In Australia, the Democratic Labor party was formed in 1956 by a mainly Catholic splinter group from the Australian Labor party. Though some bishops favoured it, others did not, and opinion polls indicate that only a minority of Catholics supported it.[1] In Quebec, the *Union nationale* was a major party in provincial politics from the nineteen-thirties to the nineteen-sixties, with a programme based on Catholic social teaching and receiving initially much support from the clergy, but in later years the latter were alienated by its record of corruption.[2] In the United Kingdom, the Irish Nationalist party performed some of the functions of a Catholic party during its heyday (1885–1918). Its electoral support was overwhelmingly Catholic, and it was entrusted by the bishops of both Ireland and England with the protection of Catholic interests in the House of Commons.[3] To the party, however, this role was incidental and indeed slightly embarrassing: it was always anxious to show – for instance, by putting forward Protestant candidates whenever possible – that its appeal was national and not denominational. The other examples of what might conceivably be called Catholic parties that I have come across have all been at local or regional level: Archbishop Hughes's slate of dissident Democrats in the New York elections of 1842; the Catholic Representation Committee in Belfast (independent of the Irish Nationalist party) in the eighteen-nineties; the Centre party in Liverpool municipal politics during the nineteen-twenties; the Democratic party in New South Wales at the same date; the Nationalist party in Northern Ireland and its offshoots, from the nineteen-twenties to the present.

By and large, Catholics in the Anglo-American world have preferred to support one of the major parties in their respective countries, rather than set up parties of their own. This does not mean that they have no preference between the major parties. Survey and ecological evidence shows that they have disproportionately supported the Democrats in the United States, the Liberals in Canada, Liberals and then Labour in Britain and New Zealand, Labor in Australia. Only in Ireland, an overwhelmingly Catholic country, is it impossible to distinguish any of the three main parties as being more Catholic than the others. Nevertheless, even if Catholics in Anglo-American countries tend to favour one party against another, this is a far cry from the confessional parties of continental Europe.

The same distinction can be seen in the field of social organisations. Continental Europe has been the stronghold of the denominational organisations. Catholic trade unions are stronger than any other group in Belgium; they run second to the communist-controlled unions in Italy and to the socialist-controlled ones in Switzerland. In the Netherlands, they used to be a close second to the socialist unions until they merged with the latter in 1976. In France, the trade unions of Catholic inspiration secularised themselves in 1964 but were, before that date, the second largest trade-union grouping. In Germany, the independent Christian (*de facto* mainly Catholic) trade unions are nowadays a small group, but they have been more important in the past; in Austria, the Christian trade unions, formerly independent, retain autonomy within the framework of a neutral trade-union federation. In Belgium, the Netherlands and Switzerland, Catholic farmers have established separate organisations of their own; in France, Italy and to a lesser extent in other countries, farmers' organisations are often Catholic in inspiration. In the Netherlands, there is a Catholic employers' organisation, which negotiates with government and trade unions in partnership with neutral and Protestant employers' associations. Youth, family and small-business organisations also exist to a varying extent on a denominational basis in these countries.

In the Anglo-American world, on the other hand, Catholics

have rarely formed distinct social organisations. Some rural self-help movements in Ireland and in both English-speaking and French-speaking Canada have been led by clergy and have been influenced by Catholic social teaching. A distinct Catholic trade-union movement was built up in Quebec, though it never organised all workers there and has now secularised itself. In Britain and the United States, associations of Catholic trade unionists have existed as ginger groups in the wider trade-union movement. In Australia, a similar ginger group – the Movement – was influential in the nineteen-fifties. Catholic employers have formed associations in Britain and the United States. But on the whole, Catholics in these countries have been remarkable for their low level of self-segregation; instead they have joined the national trade unions and other social organisations, and have often reached important positions within them.

As far as clerical activity is concerned, the distinction between two groups of countries may be less marked. At any rate in the past, priests in the Anglo-American world have sometimes given vigorous leadership to their people. This has been most obvious in Ireland and Quebec, but there have been examples elsewhere. Archbishop Hughes of New York in the eighteen-forties, Archbishop Ireland of St Paul in the eighteen-eighties, Cardinal Manning of Westminster in the same period, Archbishop Mannix of Melbourne during the First World War and again in the nineteen-fifties – all these and others besides have been notable figures in the politics of their respective countries. On the whole, however, the clergy have been more circumspect about engaging in politics in the Anglo-American world than they have been in continental Europe. In all the continental countries under study, the clergy have played an important part in organising confessional parties and social organisations. They have also played an important part in drumming up electoral support for Christian Democratic parties. Through the nineteen-fifties and most of the sixties, it was routine for the hierarchies of West Germany, Italy, Belgium and the Netherlands to publish pastoral letters before elections, which in effect amounted to a recommendation to vote Christian Democrat. The Austrian and French hierarchies were relatively circumspect after 1945, but at an earlier period they, too, had a period of active political leadership. Only the Swiss hierarchy has a long-standing tradition of reticence.

The continent has also been the home of the priest-deputy. True, this phenomenon is now almost a thing of the past; but there was a time in the nineteen-twenties when priests led the Catholic parties in three countries (Mgr Kaas in Germany, Mgr Nolens in the Netherlands, Mgr Seipel in Austria); while the secretary and moving spirit, if not the formal leader, of the equivalent party in Italy was also a priest (Fr Luigi Sturzo). Among Anglo-American countries, on the other hand, the United States Congress has only twice had priest-members, one elected in 1822 and the other in 1970.[4] The latter, Father Robert F. Drinan, was required by the Vatican not to stand again at the 1980 elections. Priests do not seem ever to have served in the legislatures of the Commonwealth countries or of Ireland, though Cardinal Moran of Sydney stood unsuccessfully in 1897 for the Australian constitutional convention. In the United Kingdom, this abstention could be explained as due to a legislative bar included in the Catholic Emancipation Act of 1829; but that measure did not apply to the British colonies or the United States. If priests have seldom run for office in Anglo-American countries, the cause has lain in a Church policy distinct from that on the continent.

There are, to be sure, variations within both groups of countries. In continental Europe, closed Catholicism was taken to its greatest extent in the Netherlands and Belgium during the period roughly 1920–60. Here virtually the whole Catholic population was mobilised behind parties of explicitly Catholic orientation, with the names 'Catholic' or 'Christian' in their titles. These parties were linked with an impressive array of Catholic social organisations – trade unions, farmers' movements, insurance and welfare organisations, and many more. The hierarchies intervened repeatedly to denounce breakaway groups and maintain Catholic unity. On the other hand, closed Catholicism has been least evident in France. Except for a brief period after the Second World War, it has always been impossible to impose unity on French Catholics. A deep fissure, going right back to the French Revolution, has always divided them into those who favour conciliating the dominant forces of the age and those who favour intransigence; and under one pair of labels or another the conflict has constantly recurred. Other countries in continental Europe have fallen somewhere between the French and the Belgo-Dutch extremes. The two nearest approaches to a closed Catholicism after Belgium and the Netherlands are to be found in Austria between the wars and in Italy since 1945.

There are variations, too, within the Anglo-American countries. French Canada in the nineteen-forties and fifties developed a Catholicism almost as closed as that of continental Europe, with confessional social organisations, a fair degree of political involvement by the clergy, and – at provincial level – a party of Catholic inspiration. Quebec, however, was only part of a country then (whatever may happen in the future), and Canadian Catholics as a whole maintained a fairly 'open' aspect. Even in Quebec, Catholics voted at federal elections for nationwide, catch-all parties, appealing to Protestants as well as Catholics. The countries nearest the open end of the spectrum have perhaps been Britain and New Zealand, with Australia, Ireland and the United States occupying intermediate positions. However, when every variation within the two groups of countries is taken into account, it is still the contrast between the two groups as a whole which stands out.

The question then arises: why has Catholicism been nearer the closed end of the spectrum in continental Europe than in the Anglo-American world? One explanation can be ruled out at the start: that Catholics in the Anglo-American world have been on better terms with their fellow-countrymen than Catholics in continental Europe. The record makes such a hypothesis hard to sustain. In the United Kingdom of Great Britain and Ireland, the demand for Catholic emancipation aroused bitter opposition until it was reluctantly conceded in 1829. There followed conflicts over the government grant to Maynooth seminary (1845), the establishment of a Catholic hierarchy in England (1850), and state aid to Catholic schools (recurrently, but especially round 1902). The stubborn opposition to self-government for Ireland, not overcome until

1921, had religious overtones. In Northern Ireland, tensions between religious groups continue till this day. In Australia and New Zealand, the problem of whether to grant state aid to denominational schools caused intense controversy, especially in the eighteen-seventies; and during and after the First World War, the Irish nationalist sympathies of most Australasian Catholics caused a cleavage between them and their fellow-citizens of British extraction. In Canada, the question of denominational education caused recurrent difficulties, probably most acute at the time of the Manitoba schools crisis in the eighteen-nineties. Differing attitudes to the war effort during the First and Second World Wars caused difficulties between French and English-speaking Canadians and therefore, to some extent, between Catholic and Protestant. In the United States, Catholic immigration caused recurrent waves of protest from a Protestant majority afraid of being swamped. The worst of these crises occurred in the eighteen-fifties, when a wave of sectarian riots swept America and an anti-Catholic party, the Know-Nothings, won many votes. There was another wave of resentment in the late nineteenth century (the era of the American Protective Association) and again in the nineteen-twenties (when the Klu Klux Klan was anti-Catholic as much as anti-black). Since then relations have improved, but even in the forties and fifties some American Protestants showed much suspicion of the Catholic Church.[5]

It is true that there has also been much bitterness in the countries of continental Europe. In Switzerland, there was a civil war between Catholic and Protestant cantons in 1847, which was followed by decades in which Catholics felt themselves a beaten minority. In Germany, Catholics endured a period of oppression, the *Kulturkampf,* in the eighteen-seventies, during which hundreds of priests were imprisoned or exiled and various legal restrictions imposed on the Church. In the Netherlands, relations were calmer; but even there reports of a possible restoration of the Catholic hierarchy provoked a wave of anti-Catholic demonstrations in 1841; and the actual establishment of such a hierarchy produced an even bigger wave of protest in 1853. In the nominally Catholic countries – France, Italy, Austria and

Belgium – the traditional power and status of the Church provoked widespread resentment, and during the second half of the nineteenth century and the early part of the twentieth it was at times the most important single issue in politics. In Italy, the Vatican refused for decades to have any formal relations with the state. In France, the expropriation of church property in 1906 produced a wave of demonstrations and protests. In Austria, tension between clerical and anti-clerical issued finally in the civil war of 1934. However, it would be difficult to demonstrate that these tensions were clearly worse than those in the Anglo-American world: that, say, the *Kulturkampf* indicated a higher level of hostility than the wave of sectarian riots which spread across America in the eighteen-fifties. The truth is that in both groups of countries Catholicism has in the past aroused intense suspicion and bitterness.

Another possible explanation is that all depends on the relative strength of Catholics in the two groups of countries. It could be argued that where Catholics are weak, they have no hope of remedying grievances by building up closed organisations of their own: their only hope is to work with other groups in broader coalitions. A parallel might be found in the behaviour of Jews, who have, to put it mildly, aroused as much antagonism as Catholics; but (with exceptions in pre-1914 Austria and post-1918 Poland) they have not attempted to counter it by building up parties of their own: they have been too small a minority for that to be practicable. At the other end of the scale, where Catholics predominate, there is no need for them to build up a closed Catholicism. Every political party and every social organisation will automatically take account of Catholic susceptibilities. It will not even be necessary for the clergy to intervene in politics, because the politicians will share their values. It is only when Catholics are in an intermediate band of strength that the construction of a closed Catholicism becomes both practicable and profitable. In such circumstances, Catholics are strong enough to maintain themselves as a separate force, yet weak enough to need to do so.

There is a good deal of force in this explanation. If we plot the relative strength of practising Catholics in the different

Table 1. Estimates of the proportion of practising Catholics in the population of different countries (Anglo-American countries are in italics.)

Country	Approx. percentage of practising Catholics	
Ireland	85	
Belgium	48	
Italy	43	
Canada	37	
Quebec		75
Rest of Canada		19
Austria	36	
The Netherlands	32	
France	23	
West Germany	23	
Switzerland	21	
United States	16	
Australia	13	
New Zealand	9	
Great Britain	6	

Data relate to about 1960. The material on which this table is based is described in Appendix B. It must be stressed that the figures offered are only approximate. For a number of countries they may be in error by several percentage points. All that this table offers is an indication of the order of magnitude of the figures for different countries.

countries under consideration (as is attempted in Table 1), we find that in continental Europe practising Catholics are indeed in the intermediate band of strength – roughly twenty to fifty per cent – where a closed Catholicism is most viable. Anglo-American countries, on the other hand, are with one exception divided between countries where Catholicism is either overwhelmingly strong (Ireland) or rather weak (United States, Australia, New Zealand, United Kingdom). The deviant case is Canada, with practising Catholics making up about 37 per cent of the population. But Canada consists of two contrasting areas: Quebec, where practising Catholics are second only to Ireland in proportionate strength, and the remaining provinces, where the proportion of practising Catholics is closer to that of the other English-speaking countries. It could be argued, then, that an open Catholicism is less inappropriate to it than would appear if we simply considered the national figures.

However, the proportionate-balance explanation does not entirely meet the case. There are areas in the Anglo-American world where Catholics would be strong enough to sustain a closed Catholicism if they wished to do so. Examples might be the states of lower New England – Massachusetts, Rhode Island and Connecticut – or the Canadian province of New Brunswick. An even more striking example is Northern Ireland, where practising Catholics muster around thirty per cent of the population and where Catholic-Protestant tensions are severe. Though Northern Ireland Catholics display a highly distinctive political behaviour, it cannot be described as a closed Catholicism. The principal parties drawing their support from the Catholic minority claim to be nationalist, not Catholic, parties. The major social organisations, such as trade unions, are not organised on denominational lines. It has been rare for priests or bishops to intervene in politics – much rarer than in some parts of the continent. Clearly, some other factor besides the right numerical strength is required before a closed Catholicism will develop in a given area.

Another approach might be to explain the difference between continental Europe and Anglo-America in terms of their overall political culture. For it is not just Catholics who differ in their political behaviour between the two groups of countries: other groups differ as well. In continental Europe, it might be said that a closed Catholicism has been faced by a closed socialism, a closed communism, even a closed Protestantism. In Belgium, Germany, Austria, the Netherlands and Switzerland, powerful Socialist parties have built up a sub-culture of their own, in which parties and social organisations provide – or at least in the past provided – for the bulk of their members' needs. In France and Italy, strong Communist parties perform the same role. In the Netherlands, the more fundamentalist Protestants have developed a similar sub-culture, with their own political parties and social organisations. The Anglo-American countries, on the other hand, are more homogeneous. All of them tend towards a two-party system in which two major parties compete to weld diverse groups into a winning coalition. Social organisations such as trade unions and employers' federations also seek as comprehensive a membership as possible. Catholic political behaviour in both groups of countries reflects the general political behaviour of the society. What needs to be explained, then, is not the differences between Catholics in the two groups of countries, but the differences between the two groups of countries as a whole. Why should Anglo-American societies be so much more homogeneous and European ones so much more fragmented?

This approach is attractive, but it, too, has a drawback. The difficulty lies in finding a general theory to explain the contrast. The classification of western democracies into Anglo-American and continental European is one which several political scientists have found useful.[6] The pioneer was Gabriel Almond, who in an influential article published in 1956 drew attention to the contrast between the homogeneous political cultures of the Anglo-American countries and the fragmented cultures of continental Europe.[7] Though he described the distinction in this preliminary survey, he did not seek to explain it. Subsequent researchers, instead of explaining the differences between Almond's categories, have found it more profitable to refine the categories themselves. Sartori and Lijphart have stressed the contrast between France and Italy, with their deep political cleavages, and the Low Countries or Scandinavia, with their multi-party but cohesive systems.[8] Lipset and Rokkan have developed a model for explaining differences between European party systems which is extraordinarily fertile, but entails grouping European countries into eight different categories.[9] For their own purposes, the distinctions developed by these writers are accurate and satisfying, but they do not go far towards explaining the big contrast in *Catholic* politics – which is between continental Europe as a whole and Anglo-America.

To seek to explain differences in the political behaviour of Catholics in terms of differences in the political culture of their countries may, however, be pushing the search for explanations unnecessarily far; for Catholic history has an autonomy of its own. As we shall see in subsequent chapters, the political behaviour of Catholics in different situations can largely be explained in terms of developments within Catholicism. Indeed, a case can be made for saying that Catholic history is crucial for explaining larger variations in political culture, rather than vice versa. For when the history of the various European countries is examined, it emerges that in most of them the Catholic sub-culture was the first to crystallise. The Netherlands is the only exception : there, the Calvinist sub-culture emerged at least as early. Elsewhere on the continent, a closed socialism or a closed communism emerged only after a closed Catholicism was already developing.

Three explanations of the differences between Catholicism in Anglo-America and in continental Europe have so far been discussed – that they are due to differences in the level of hostility between Catholics and others; that they are due to differences in the balance of numbers; and that they are due to differences in the wider political culture. The first can be ruled out as incorrect. The second has merit, but must be regarded as a necessary rather than a sufficient condition for the contrast to arise. The third is ideally the best explanation, but in the absence of a general theory to explain the differences in the wider political culture, we shall have to get on without it.

However, all the theories we have so far discussed have one weakness: by concentrating on differences between groups of countries, they fail to take account of the degree to which both groups of countries have pursued a common course of development. For the differences between Anglo-America and continental Europe are not absolute; they are more a matter of differing degrees in the emphasis of trends. When we compare their histories, the following facts emerge.

1. If we go back far enough – say to before 1870 – the distinction between the closed Catholicism of the continent and the open Catholicism of the Anglo-American world disappears. Catholic political parties did not yet exist or were only embryonic. Catholic social organisations had hardly begun to form. The Catholic clergy were not generally active in politics; they were equally likely to be active in an Anglo-American country as in a European

one. Catholics in both Anglo-America and continental Europe were clustered near the open end of the spectrum.

2. If we come close enough to the present, we find that the two groups of countries are converging again. Catholicism in continental Europe is no longer as closed as it was in, say, 1960. The Christian Democratic parties have become less powerful, or less confessional, or both. The same has happened to most of the Catholic social organisations. The clergy are less active politically or, if active, are more divided. Anglo-American Catholics, near the open end of the spectrum, are being increasingly imitated by the Catholics of continental Europe.
3. Thus the contrast between continental Europe and the Anglo-American countries is historically contingent. It is not an immutable contrast, but largely concentrated in one period, roughly 1870–1960.
4. Even when the contrast between the two groups of countries is at its greatest, it can be exaggerated. In the late nineteenth and early twentieth centuries, Catholics in both groups of countries were moving towards the closed end of the spectrum. Even in the Anglo-American world, some Catholic social organisations were established, though not so many as in Europe. In some countries, notably Ireland and Canada, the clergy played an active role in politics. There were even a few attempts, admittedly not very successful, to establish Catholic political parties. The difference between the two groups of countries in these years was one of pace, rather than direction. Both moved in the direction of closed Catholicism, but continental Europe moved further and faster than Anglo-America.

Thus, any explanation of the conditions in which closed or open Catholicism prevail must take account of variations over time as well as variations over space. Contrasts between the same country at different periods need to be considered, as well as contrasts between different countries at the same period. Indeed, variations over time matter more. Consequently, their analysis will take up the bulk of the discussion in this book. To them, the next four chapters will be devoted.

Just one point of terminology must be stressed before the discussion is taken further. The terms 'continental Europe' and 'Anglo America', which will be repeatedly used, have a precise meaning in this book. They refer to the two groups, of seven and six countries respectively, listed at the beginning of this chapter. They have no wider application.

2

Variations over time: The beginnings of closed Catholicism, c. 1790–1870

The beginnings of closed Catholicism in the countries under consideration in this book can be traced back to the end of the eighteenth century. The key event was the French Revolution, which began in 1789. The revolutionaries were not at first anti-Catholic, but their initial attack on the privileges of crown and nobility soon carried over into an attack on the Church, and by the early seventeen-nineties one of the preconditions for the emergence of closed Catholicism was present: the existence of a dispute sharply marking out Catholics from their opponents. The issue was eventually compromised by a concordat between the papacy and the French government in 1801, but the divisions between clerical and anti-clerical which opened up in French society during the seventeen-nineties continued, through many changes of regime, to be a factor in French politics right down to the present day. Meanwhile the spread of the principles of revolution by the victories of the French revolutionary army ensured that the same cleavage appeared in many other continental countries. In parts of the Anglo-American world kept safe by the British navy from French conquest, Catholic demands for religious equality had a somewhat similar polarising effect.

Of the three components in closed Catholicism – Catholic parties, Catholic social organisations, and political activity by the clergy – the last-named was historically the first to appear. The earliest example of clerical electioneering that I have noted comes from 1797, when French Catholic clergy were reported to be active on behalf of royalist candidates in the first elections under the Directory. Local examples are reported from Quebec as early as 1800[1] and from Ireland as early as 1807.[2] In both countries, clerical electioneering was becoming widespread by the eighteen-twenties. In France, the tradition of clerical electioneering revived under the Bourbon monarchy, and in 1830, when the fate of Charles X's regime was trembling in the balance, there was a determined attempt by some bishops to influence the results of the general election. According to one historian, 'the terms used in some of these pastoral letters and sermons quite outdo any other clerical utterances of France in the nineteenth century.'[3] The greatest degree of clerical electioneering in the first half of the nineteenth century appears to have been reached in Belgium, where the clergy – under the direction of their bishops – exercised a systematic control over the choice of candidates and the canvassing and polling of electors.[4]

The same period saw the emergence of the priest-deputy. Clerical membership of *upper* houses was of long standing. From medieval times, the Church had ranked as one of the estates of the realm, and thus where estates survived, churchmen were assured of representation. In the early nineteenth century, Catholic prelates sat in the upper houses of the parliaments of France and several German states. The innovation was to have clergy being elected as representatives of the people at large. Several Catholic priests were elected to the Dutch national assembly of 1796. In Belgium, thirteen of the 200 members of the constituent assembly of 1830 were priests. In the French constituent assembly of 1848, three bishops and twelve priests were among those elected. In the Austrian *Reichstag* of the same year, there were twenty clergy. Thirteen Catholic clergy sat in the Frankfurt *Vorparlament* of 1848 (representing all Germany), and twenty-eight in the Prussian national assembly of the same year.

As far as Catholic parties are concerned, the first political party to call itself by that name appeared in Belgium at the end of the eighteen-twenties. A little earlier in the decade, the Catholic Association in Ireland carried out many of the functions of a political party. Catholics in the parliaments of Baden and Württemberg were taking concerted political action from the late eighteen-thirties, and German Catholics acted to some extent as a party in the Frankfurt *Vorparlament* of 1848.

Catholic social organisations, of the kind that later provided such an important underpinning to Catholic parties, can also be traced back to the same period. In the France of the eighteen-twenties, a society called the *Congrégation* sought by a network of local clubs, charitable ventures and newspapers to re-establish the influence of Christianity in society. In the eighteen-forties, a German priest, Adolf Kolping, started a welfare movement for young Catholic workers which spread to Austria, Switzerland and the Netherlands. This is generally considered a forerunner of the Catholic labour movement. In 1839, Frederic Ozanam founded the Saint Vincent de Paul Society, which soon spread all over the world. Though strictly charitable and non-political, this society provided a means whereby Catholics learnt co-operative action for social ends.

However, compared with what was to come, the striking feature of the situation around mid-century was the relative lack of development of a closed Catholicism anywhere. There are many reasons for this. One is that the political preconditions did not yet exist in many countries. A closed Catholicism – i.e. the organisation of Catholics as a distinct sub-culture – requires a certain minimum of political freedoms. One cannot have a Catholic political party unless political parties in general are free to organise. One cannot have Catholic social organisations unless social organisations in general are free to develop. One cannot have clerical guidance over the political behaviour of Catholics unless bishops are reasonably free to communicate with their flocks, which entails a certain degree of freedom of the press. In short, a closed Catholicism is possible only where there is an open society.

Now although the Anglo-American countries could be classified as open societies by the mid-nineteenth century, much of continental Europe could not. Freedom of the press, of assembly, and of association was restricted by law or by various administrative devices. These restrictions were severe in Austria and most of Italy, considerable in France and most parts of Germany, least in Belgium, the Netherlands and Switzerland. Where they did exist, it was difficult for parties and social organisations, whether Catholic or other, to flourish.

Another obstacle to the development of a closed Catholicism in many countries – both European and Anglo-American – was the electoral system. Unless the electorate is large and elections fairly secure from rigging by the government, party organisation (whether Catholic or other) is unlikely to develop. A survey of the situation about 1852 – after the gains temporarily won in several countries during the 1848 revolutions had been rescinded – shows that this condition was largely lacking. In Belgium, the Netherlands, and the kingdom of Sardinia, only two to three per cent of the population had the right to vote. In the United Kingdom, the proportion was about six per cent. In Prussia, many could vote, but the electoral system was so constructed that the wealthy minority outweighed the poor majority. In Austria and the states of Italy outside Sardinia, there were no elections at all. France had manhood suffrage, but elections were so controlled by the government that opposition was almost stifled. Switzerland had manhood suffrage too, but, following their defeat in the civil war of 1847, Catholics had been gerrymandered out of government in several cantons where they had a majority. The British colonies in North America and Australasia had a wide suffrage, but populations so small that elaborate party organisation was unnecessary. The only country in the world where mass party organisation existed as early as the eighteen-fifties was the United States.

Not only were political pre-conditions for a closed Catholicism widely lacking, but so were social pre-conditions. A closed Catholicism (or a closed anything else) presupposes a certain minimum of social and economic development. Even if the forms of constitutional government exist, they will not be used to the full if these other conditions are not present. Trade unions, for instance, are likely to flourish only where an urban working class is a sizeable proportion of the population and has reached the level of prosperity and self-awareness where it can throw up leaders from its own ranks. In most of the countries under discussion in this book, these conditions had not been fulfilled by the mid-nineteenth century. Industrialisation was in its infancy, except in Britain, Belgium, and parts of France and Germany; much of the urban population was wretchedly poor. Farmers, too, were in most countries only just beginning to reach the level of affluence and self-awareness where they began to see the need for and the possibility of organisation. Moreover, the prevailing ethos of laissez-faire limited the need for organised interest groups. One of the main purposes of such groups in modern times is to influence government policy. When governments did not have a policy over wide areas of economic life, there was obviously less need to influence them.

There was a further reason for the slow growth of closed Catholicism. This was that older traditions in the Catholic Church about how to handle political controversies were still strong. During centuries of experience, churchmen had built up a battery of instruments for use in their relations with politicians. The one most favoured was direct negotiation between Church and government. Negotiation went on in private, so that no one's *amour propre* was exposed to rebuff, and much use was made of legal forms and historical precedents. This technique often led to success. It was frequently used in the early nineteenth century, which saw a large crop of concordats – that is, of treaties negotiated between the papacy and a secular government, whereby the rights of the Church were given legal guarantees.

If direct negotiation failed, a second weapon was what can be described as the 'dramatic gesture', in which churchmen used passive resistance against the regime with which they were in conflict. The most famous example in the early nineteenth century was that of Pope Pius VII. Rather than give in to what he considered unreasonable demands from Napoleon, the pope allowed himself to be imprisoned and then caused Napoleon much embarrassment by refusing to make any episcopal appointments or transact any other business until he was released. Another example came from Prussia in the eighteen-thirties. Archbishop Droste zu Vischering of Cologne, finding himself in conflict with the government over the law relating to mixed marriage, did not attempt to organise political opposition. Instead he contented himself with a public protest. The government imprisoned him, and the consequent reaction among the Catholic Rhinelanders proved as effective as a political campaign might have done. The government was forced in due course to release the archbishop and negotiate a compromise.

If these two methods failed, a third was available as a last resort – that of armed rebellion. In the nineteenth century, churchmen were hesitant about or hostile to the use of this method, even in extreme circumstances. The French Revolution had proved what horrors could be unleashed once constituted authority was defied. The papacy had a special reason for discountenancing revolt, because it might be used as a precedent against its own rule in the Papal States. Not surprisingly, then, the clergy could often be among the strongest opponents of revolt – as French Canadians found out in 1837, or Irish in 1867. None the less, there were plenty of precedents from the middle ages and from reformation times for churchmen commending rebellion against what was considered intolerable tyranny; and even in the nineteenth century, the right of rebellion was never entirely renounced. It was repeatedly applied by Catholic populations, even if their clergy were ambivalent or opposed. In continental Europe and Anglo-America, we find in the period 1790–1870 the following episodes in which the insurgents claimed the defence of the Catholic faith as being part, at least, of their motivation: the Vendée (1793), Ireland (1798), Belgium (1798), the Sanfedisti (1799), the Tyrol (1808), Belgium (1830), and the Swiss Sonderbund (1847). If we were to go outside these countries to Spain, Latin America or Poland, we should find several more examples.

A Catholic population with a grievance had, then, a number of weapons at its disposal. The development of closed Catholicism was simply an addition to the armoury, and in the early stages it was unclear how valuable it might be. Indeed, in the eyes of some churchmen, it was imprudent and even unjust to encourage too much organisation by the laity: imprudent, because it might mean that bishops' authority over their flocks would be weakened by that of lay political leaders; unjust, because it might arouse among the laity a lack of due deference to the civil authority. Considerations such as these led, for instance, some French bishops to oppose the establishment of a Catholic party in France during the eighteen-forties and some Prussian bishops to deprecate the establishment of such a party in their country during the eighteen-fifties. As late as 1872, when the *Kulturkampf* was getting under way, a bishop such as Hoffstätter of Passau could argue against defending the Church's rights by political means, preferring to rely on the law.[5] Support by the Church for a closed Catholicism was a slow and uncertain growth.

There was yet another reason why closed Catholicism was slow in developing. The necessary cleavage between Catholics and others was not sufficiently sharp. This may seem a surprising judgment, when histories of the nineteenth century are full of conflicts between Catholics and others, but a brief survey of the state of politics during the second quarter of the nineteenth century will make the point clear.

During these years, two main political tendencies could be found almost everywhere in the countries under consideration: liberal and conservative. True, the distinction must not be drawn too sharply. The primitive nature of party organisation, and the mixed views of many people near the centre of the political spectrum, meant that not everyone could be easily categorised under one label or the other. Moreover, the precise views of conservatives and liberals could vary between one country and another, or between different kinds of conservative and liberal even within the same country. None the less, the distinction is broadly valid. Furthermore, one can generalise roughly about what liberals and conservatives stood for in the countries under consideration taken as a group.

Liberals, as their name implied, stood for an increase of liberty. They held an implicitly optimistic view of human nature. They believed that human beings, if freed from external constraints, were likely to evolve in a desirable direction, becoming more harmonious, tolerant and fulfilled. They sought to reduce the power of privileged bodies, such as monarchies, established churches, and hereditary aristocracies. Instead they called for governments responsible to elected parliaments. Where the franchise was narrow, they generally stood for its extension. They called for legal equality between man and man, which brought with it religious equality, the abolition of political censorship, and freedom of speech and of association. Economically, they favoured the free play of market forces and international free trade. In some countries – notably Germany, Austria and Switzerland – they stood for centralisation, believing that local particularisms obstructed the spread of liberty. They were strongest among the growing urban middle class.

The views of conservatives cannot be summarised so easily. Few of them believed that liberal demands could be met with a flat negative. Their reservations were more about the pace of change than its direction. Yet they tended to a more pessimistic view of human nature and believed that, freed of constraint, men were as likely to degenerate as to develop. They considered that ancient and respected institutions – monarchies, aristocracies, established churches, traditional units such as German principalities or Swiss cantons – were part of the cement which held society together and deserved preservation. On social and economic matters they were often as progressive as liberals. They were less worried about interfering with market forces and were often genuinely concerned for the welfare of the poor, in a paternalistic sort of way. They also tended to be more sensitive than liberals to the special needs of agriculture. They were strongest, naturally enough, among monarchs and aristocrats; but they could also mobilise considerable support among the peasantry.

As a global generalisation, one can say that of these two tendencies Catholics were more likely to support the conservative. As adherents of a faith deeply committed to the doctrine of original sin, Catholics found it difficult to accept the optimistic view of human nature which liberal ideology implied. The liberal doctrine of religious equality provoked theological objections: it meant that the one true Church of Christ was being put on a par with man-made religions or, worse, with atheism. In much of continental Europe, there was an additional reason for mistrusting liberals: they stood for hostility to established churches. In most of this area, the Catholic Church *was* the established church. Thus the liberal doctrine could be construed to imply an attack on Catholicism. Particularly in the early years after the Restoration of 1815, the link between Catholicism and conservatism was strongly marked.

However, it should not be thought that all Catholics were instinctively drawn to conservatism. To be a conservative meant not just standing up for the privileges of the Church: it meant standing also for the privileges of monarchs and aristocrats. This was attractive for those Catholics who happened to be monarchs or aristocrats; but it was not so compelling for the much larger numbers who were not. On the contrary, they might feel that their interests – not just their economic or social interests, but also their interests as Catholics – might be better served by adopting parts of the liberal programme. The liberal principles of freedom of the press, assembly and association could benefit Catholics as well as others. The extension of the franchise could in many countries produce an extension of Catholic influence, if masses of Catholic peasants joined the electorate.

Moreover, the experience of Catholics under conservative regimes was not uniformly favourable. Such regimes tended to protect the Church against its enemies by prosecutions for blasphemy, by censoring the press and by giving financial aid, but they also demanded a great measure of control over the Church. They wanted the major say in the appointing of bishops. They claimed the right to control communication between the bishops and the Vatican, and between the bishops and their flocks. They obstructed the creation of new dioceses and parishes to take account of shifting populations. There was a good case for saying that this tutelage damaged the Church, which would be better off in a framework of equal freedom for all, such as the liberals demanded.

For all these reasons a growing liberal Catholic movement was to be found, beginning in the eighteen-twenties and lasting through the thirties and forties. Its most extreme exponent, the French priest Félicité de Lamennais, was condemned by the pope in 1834 and subsequently left the Church; but Lamennais' followers, Montalembert and Lacordaire, continued as Catholics in good standing to propagate his views. Meanwhile Daniel O'Connell in Ireland and the Catholic leaders in Belgium continued in practice to do what Lamennais had advocated in principle; to use liberal freedoms in defence of Catholic interests. Almost everywhere, both in continental Europe and in Anglo-America, groups of liberal Catholics existed. On the whole they were strongest in English-speaking countries and in the Netherlands, where

Catholicism had not been an established church. They were weaker in France and Germany, weaker still in Austria and Italy; but they were to be found everywhere.[6] The peak of the liberal Catholic movement was reached in 1848, when Catholics co-operated in working the parliamentary institutions which were set up in many European countries during that year; and when, in return, revolutionaries showed themselves far more friendly to religion than their predecessors had done in the seventeen-nineties. The old equation of Catholic and conservative had widely broken down, and Catholics seemed to be found as often on the liberal side in politics as on the conservative. At that point, the possibility of Catholics building themselves up into a cohesive sub-culture must have seemed more remote that ever. They were too much dispersed along the political spectrum for the minimum necessary unity to be achieved.

In the remainder of this chapter, I shall examine developments in the political behaviour of Catholics during the period 1850–70. In only one country did these twenty years show any marked advance towards the development of a closed Catholicism. This was Prussia, which had a Protestant monarchy and an overwhelmingly Protestant bureaucracy, but a one-third Catholic population. In the eighteen-forties, Catholics had felt that they were not getting a square deal from the Prussian regime and tended to collaborate with the Liberals. During the fifties and sixties, however, Catholics and Liberals diverged. Liberals favoured the introduction of civil marriage and secular education, which Catholics opposed; they favoured the unification of Italy, while Catholics rallied to the defence of the Pope's temporal power; above all, they differed from Catholics in their attitude to German unification. Most Catholics wanted such unification to include Austria, which would give Catholics a majority in a united Germany; most Liberals preferred to exclude Austria, which they considered a backward clerical state. On the other hand, Catholics could not simply go over to the Conservatives, whom they considered at heart opposed to the guarantee of religious equality enshrined in the Prussian constitution of 1850. Moreover, Prussian Conservatives were almost as anti-

Austrian as Prussian Liberals. There was nothing for it, then, but to organise as a separate group, and from 1852 a distinct Catholic party existed in the Prussian parliament. At no time did this party include all Catholic deputies, and it collapsed altogether in 1866, but it formed the basis for a tradition. In 1870, on the foundation of the German Empire, it was replaced by a much more long-lasting successor, the Centre party.

In the other countries of continental Europe, the main development of the fifties and sixties was that the old equation between Catholic and conservative began to re-emerge. Several reasons for this can be discerned. One was the increasing dogmatism of certain liberals. In the twenties, thirties and forties, liberals had most often been interested in specific constitutional reforms. They asked for measures such as parliamentary government, freedom of the press, extensions of the franchise. These were issues on which many Catholics could agree with them; but as the fifties wore on, the more militant liberals made more far-reaching demands. Influenced by the growing prestige of science, they became more hostile to the whole range of inherited institutions and more convinced that unaided human reason could design a better alternative. They came to see the biggest obstacle to human progress as the churches, and in particular the Catholic Church, because they kept the masses in superstition.

Increasing dogmatism among liberals was accompanied by increasing dogmatism among the Catholic authorities. Pope Pius IX had shown some liberal leanings when he was first elected in 1846; but the experiences of the Italian revolution in 1848 had burnt these out of him, and in the fifties and sixties he could fairly be labelled as reactionary. In 1864, he issued the *Syllabus of Errors,* a comprehensive denunciation of liberal doctrines such as freedom of speech, freedom of the press, and freedom of worship. It ended with a ringing condemnation of the idea that 'the Holy Roman Pontiff can and ought to reconcile himself to what is called progress, liberty and modern civilisation'. In 1870, the First Vatican Council proclaimed the dogma of papal infallibility, i.e. the doctrine that in certain circumstances the pope is protected by the Holy Spirit from error. This seemed to liberals an assualt on their principle of free enquiry, and even those who had stomached the *Syllabus* of 1864 found it hard to co-operate with Catholics after the declaration of 1870.

Concurrently with philosophical disagreements, practical issues arose which made it hard for Catholics and liberals to collaborate. The most important of these was education. Since the late nineteenth century, education has so often been the main bone of contention between Catholics and others that it is surprising to find how late the issue was in rising to prominence. An anthology of papal pronouncements on the subject contains only a handful of items from before 1850.[7] Such pronouncements do not become frequent till the eighteen-seventies, and the only full-length encyclical on the subject was published as late as 1929. The first papal condemnations of specific measures date from mid-century: a condemnation of a proposed Irish university system (the Queen's Colleges) in 1847 and of a Sardinian school law in 1850.

The principal reason why education should have become an increasingly contentious issue in the second half of the nineteenth century is that education itself was expanding rapidly. Developing industry needed a literate labour force. Where elected parliaments existed, a literate electorate seemed desirable. Liberals believed that education was a good in itself, dispelling superstition and enriching lives. Conflict arose on the issue of who should provide the additional educational facilities. Liberals tended automatically to propose the state, which alone had the financial resources and which they could hope to control, through victory at parliamentary elections. Catholics tended to propose the Church, which had traditionally provided education to Catholic children. If the Church could not raise the necessary finance unaided, the solution, they argued, was for the state to assist it. To liberals, this seemed outrageous. A main reason for extending education was to reduce the power of the Church. To allow the Church to continue its control of education was to undermine the value of the change.

Education by itself, however, might not have alienated Catholics so sharply from liberals if another issue, logically unrelated, had not come to the fore at about the same time. This was the temporal power of the papacy. One of the great liberal causes was the unification of Italy. An obstacle to its achievement was the existence of the Papal State, which stretched in a belt across the middle of the peninsula. In the forties, a compromise had seemed possible; for some liberals and some Catholics explored the possibility of having an Italian confederation with the pope as its head. By the fifties, neither side was interested in this solution, and a liberal victory became possible only at the Church's expense.

The issue of the temporal power remained important for a comparatively brief period. It did not become acute until 1859–60, when Italian unification – hitherto a distant dream – suddenly took a giant leap forward. Most of the peninsula was united, leaving the anomaly of the Papal State much more obtrusive than before. The issue reached its climax only a decade later, when in 1870 Italian forces annexed what was left of the Papal State. It was largely played out before the end of the seventies, by which time Catholics in most countries – though not the pope himself – had accepted the loss of the temporal power as a *fait accompli*. But while it lasted, the issue had an importance which extended far beyond Italy. On the one side, liberals applauded the unification of Italy. On the other side, many loyal Catholics felt it their duty to support the pope. After the fall of Rome in 1870, the efforts of Catholics in several countries – most notably France and Germany – to persuade their governments to restore the temporal power by force was a contentious issue in politics.

The effect of these issues was to destroy co-operation between liberals and Catholics. The date of the break varied, but at some time between the eighteen-forties and the eighteen-seventies it is to be found in all the countries of continental Europe. The change came earliest in Switzerland. Liberals had become an active force in Switzerland during the eighteen-thirties, when a movement called the Regeneration swept many Swiss cantons, overthrowing ruling oligarchies and establishing more democratic forms of government. There was nothing inherently repugnant to Catholics in this, and the movement affected Catholic cantons as well as Protestant. However, by the eighteen-forties, tensions between Catholics and liberals were developing. Here as in other parts of Europe, liberals believed in strengthening the central government at the expense of smaller units. To Catholics, who were a minority at national level, this spelt danger: they were more secure in a situation where power was diffused to the cantons. Catholic insecurity was increased when the liberals came to be dominated by their radical wing, which began to put through anti-clerical legislation in the cantons which it controlled. This produced a reaction among Catholics. In Lucerne, for instance, Catholics used the new liberal institutions to win back control from the radicals in 1841, and installed a Conservative government. By 1847, tensions had reached a point where seven Catholic cantons formed a separate league, or *Sonderbund,* to protect their interests. This seemed to the radicals like a threat to the integrity of Switzerland, and the *Sonderbund* was broken up by force. Thereafter, the identification of Catholic and Conservative was almost complete.

Belgium followed a course somewhat similar to Switzerland's. Catholics and Liberals had not always been antagonistic. Together they had secured Belgian independence in 1830, and for its first seventeen years the new state was governed by Liberal-Catholic coalitions. The coalition broke up in 1847, largely because Liberals felt that Catholics were getting too strong a grip on education. For the next thirty years, Belgium saw a party battle, gradually increasing in intensity, between Liberals on the one hand and a party described sometimes as 'Catholic' and sometimes as 'Conservative' on the other.

Italian Catholics followed a more extreme curve. In the eighteen-fifties, the only part of Italy with representative institutions was Sardinia, where a Liberal government had a safe parliamentary majority. There were signs that Catholics were coming to accept the conventions of parliamentary government, and in the elections of 1857 they made unexpected gains. Instead of welcoming this as a sign of integration with the system, the Liberals annulled some of the elections. The more intransigent Catholics reacted by boycotting subsequent elections. This practice spread when most of Italy was united after 1860, and by 1868 was endorsed by the pope. Not all Catholics agreed with such an uncompromising stand, but the pope's instructions made it impossible for them to participate in parliamentary politics as a distinct force. The result was that the Italian parliament became an arena for competition between liberal factions. Though the term 'Conservative' was used, and indeed the governments in power between 1861 and 1876 were often labelled Conservative, the term corresponded to what would have been described as moderate liberal elsewhere. In Italy, Catholics were so conservative that they did not even support the Conservatives.

The eighteen-fifties saw a change in France, too. The *coup d'état* of 1851, which led to the establishment of the Second Empire with its strong executive and feeble parliament, was deeply distasteful to Liberals. Most Catholics, however, were opportunist. Although Napoleon III himself appears to have been a sceptic, he found it prudent to seek Catholic support for his regime. In 1850, while still President of the Second Republic, he supported the *loi Falloux* which gave the Church extensive rights in secondary education. There was a period of tension at the end of the fifties, caused by his support for Italian unification, but from 1860 to 1870 he maintained troops in Rome to support the pope's rule in his remaining dominions, and thus secured Catholic support for his regime once again. When the Second Empire collapsed in 1870, liberal Catholicism seemed a thing of the past.

In Austria, the development of political forces was masked by the weakness of parliamentary institutions till 1867. The establishment of an elected parliament led at once to a Liberal government with the twin aims of diminishing the power of the Catholic Church and centralising the state and eroding regional privileges. The first of these objectives was largely carried out in 1868–70, when civil marriage was introduced, the role of the Church in education diminished, and the concordat of 1855 denounced. These actions, however, aroused the hostility of the more strongly Catholic elements in the German-speaking population, whose representatives built up a distinct clerical or Conservative party. Among the non-German elements in Austria – Czechs, Poles, Slovenes, Italians – such anti-clerical measures might not by themselves have aroused too much hostility, for most of these groups had an anti-clerical sector among their own populations. The centralising measures of the Liberals, however, aroused the opposition of these groups, for centralisation in Austrian circumstances meant Germanisation and thus a threat to the culture of the non-German peoples. The Liberals, then, soon provoked against themselves a conservative coalition of German clericals and non-German ethnic groups, in which Catholic feeling was an important element, though only an element. By the end of the seventies, this coalition was strong enough to take power.

Friendship between Liberals and Catholics lasted longest in the Netherlands. The friendship rested on solid grounds. Though Dutch Catholics had enjoyed formal religious equality since 1795, they still held far less than their proportionate share of official positions, and the Church itself was put under various irksome restrictions. Small wonder, then, that Catholics gravitated to the Liberals, who stood for equal rights. When the Liberals forced through a reform of the constitution in 1848, they had Catholic support. Five years later, in 1853, a Liberal government permitted the establishment of a Catholic hierarchy, despite strong opposition from some Protestants. It was not until the eighteen-sixties that the Catholic-Liberal alliance beganto break down. Dutch Liberals favoured the cause of Italian unity; Dutch Catholics, on the other hand, gave the pope's defence of his temporal sovereignty exceptionally strong support, contributing proportionately more volunteers for the papal army than the Catholics of any other country. In 1868, the Dutch bishops antagonised the Liberals by calling for the establishment of denominational schools. The last straw came in 1872, when a Liberal government abolished Dutch diplomatic representation at the Holy See, thus giving countenance to the abolition of the Papal States. Dutch Catholics were by now ready for the reversal of alliances which led them to form a long-lasting coalition with evangelical Protestants.

In Anglo-American countries, however, this alienation of Catholics from Liberals did not take place. Various reasons can be suggested to explain this. One was that the factors which drove a wedge between Catholics and Liberals in Europe did not operate with the same strength in Anglo-America. True, Catholics showed some indignation over the threat to the temporal power, and in the British general election of 1859 the Liberals lost some Catholic votes on this issue. Catholics in the Anglo-American countries were too remote, too uninfluential or both to expect to influence their governments' policy on Italy, and so did not make a great issue of it. The control of education was a growing issue in Anglo-America as in Europe, and one which roused Catholic suspicions. In countries where Catholics were a minority, the demand for a secular education system was not on the whole aimed at the Catholic Church as such. Rather, it was a practical response to the problem of providing schools for a population belonging to many different churches and sects. In England, Catholics were able to form a tactical alliance with Anglicans, whose interests were not dissimilar. In Ireland and Quebec, where Catholics were the local majority, they were able to ensure the development of an education system satisfactory to themselves. Finally, Liberals in the Anglo-American world were not on the whole so dogmatic as those on the continent. They were not generally hostile to religion as such, but only to privileges being given to one church over another. Since in the Anglo-American world it was usually a Protestant church which had any privileges that might exist, this was not an obstacle to Catholic support for Liberals. Rather, it was an additional motive. In Ireland and in British colonies overseas, Catholics co-operated with Liberals to reduce the status of the Anglican church.

Catholics in the Anglo-American world had an additional reason, which did not apply on the continent of Europe, for remaining friendly with Liberals. Liberals stood for the underdog, and in Anglo-America, Catholics usually *were* the underdog. In the United States, in English Canada and in Britain, Catholics were largely recent immigrants, coming into a society already dominated by Protestants and clustering at the bottom of the social ladder. In Quebec and in Ireland, it was the Protestants who were the more recent immigrants, but penal laws or government favour had ensured them a disproportionate share of high-status positions. In the Australasian colonies Catholics had arrived together with Protestants but were grouped disproportionately in the poorer occupations. Thus, the liberal cry for greater equality was not a cause of alarm for Catholics in the Anglo-American world, but a further reason for supporting Liberal forces.

A country-by-country survey will illustrate the extent of the Liberal-Catholic alliance in the Anglo-American world. In the United Kingdom, the bulk of the Catholic population was concentrated in Ireland, and Irish Catholic constituencies voted pretty solidly for one strand or another of liberalism until the eighteen-seventies. When the change came after 1870, it was the result not of any shift to the Conservatives, but of the rise of the Irish Nationalist party. In England and Scotland, upper-class Catholics tended to Conservatism, but the bulk of the Catholic electors, even before the extension of the franchise in 1867, appear to have been immigrant Irish who sympathised with the Liberals.

In the United States, where the Democrats played the liberal role as the party of the underdog, they were also the party who attracted the bulk of the Catholic vote. Except for a small minority centred in Maryland and another small minority of recent converts, the Catholic population of the United States was composed of recent immigrants, mostly Irish or German, coming in at or near the bottom of the social scale. At the beginning of the nineteenth century, it was already noticeable that Irish Catholics tended to identify with the Jeffersonians, forerunner of the Democrats.[8] As the century wore on, events served only to increase the identification. By the eighteen-fifties, the status of the immigrant was becoming a salient issue in American politics, comparable in importance for a time to slavery. As the immigrant flood reached a height, the resentment of already established white Americans at this invasion by foreign cultures increased. Hostility was particularly directed at immigrants of Catholic faith, who posed a threat to the Protestant basis of American culture. A new party, the Know Nothings, was formed specifically to combat Catholic immigration, and for a brief period in the eighteen-fifties wielded great influence. The Republicans, who emerged in the later eighteen-fifties as the principal rival to the Democrats, also showed signs of anti-immigrant feeling. The only party in which immigrants could feel at home was the Democrats, and the party's hold on the loyalty of most American Catholics was consequently reinforced. Moreover, the Republican party, largely led by Protestant idealists, abolished slavery, fought the civil war of 1861–5, and introduced the draft. None of these actions made the Republicans popular with the immigrant masses, who feared negro competition, had no desire to fight a civil war, and perceived the draft as bearing unfairly on them. The Democratic party, on the other hand, gave immigrant Catholic politicians a ladder to power, at least at local level.[9]

In the Australasian colonies, it is harder to talk of the party identification of Catholics. Australasian historians seem agreed that, until the last two decades of the nineteenth century, it is difficult to speak of parties at all. The seven colonies – New South Wales, New Zealand, Queensland, South Australia, Tasmania, Victoria and Western Australia – still had very small populations. About 1870, these ranged from 730,000 in Victoria to only 25,000 in Western Australia. Constituencies were small: politics could largely be conducted on a face-to-face basis. In so far as they existed, parties consisted of shifting alliances of assembly members, based on personality as much as on principle. However, where liberal and conservative groupings can be detected, it seems to be the consensus among the authorities that Catholics gravitated to the liberal side.[10]

An early example of the identification of Catholic and Liberal occurred in Newfoundland. This colony, despite its poverty and small population (150,000 in 1869), developed in the mid-nineteenth century a precocious party system. Liberals stood for an end to domination by the British-appointed governor and the establishment of responsible government; Conservatives were opposed to this. The population of Newfoundland was at that date divided almost evenly between Catholics of Irish descent and Protestants of English descent. It was the Irish Catholics who provided the bulk of the support for the Liberals, while English Protestants were mostly Conservative. However, party divisions became less sharp after the Liberals secured their objective of responsible government in 1855. In the later nineteenth century, Newfoundland politics reverted to a form of group factionalism reminiscent of the Australasian colonies.[11]

There was only one part of the Anglo-American world where, in 1870, Catholics did not tend to identify with Liberals. This was in the newly-formed dominion of Canada. The contrast may be connected with the fact that Canada was the only Anglo-American country where the strongest contingent of Catholics was not provided by the Irish. In Canada, most Catholics were of French descent, and the deeply conservative nature of French-Canadian society was often remarked upon. However, a closer examination of the record shows that the contrast between Canada and the rest of the Anglo-American world was less absolute than appears at first sight. Canadian Catholics had not always been Conservatives. In the early nineteenth century, the major issue in Canadian politics had been the struggle for responsible government, and the Liberal alliance which fought for this goal comprised many French- and well as English-speaking Canadians. Even after the grant of responsible government in the eighteen-forties, French Canadians continued for a time to support the Liberals. The change in their voting habits came as late as 1854, when a growing demand for the secularisation of education – and a consequent withdrawal of state aid to Catholic schools – among the English-speaking Liberals of Canada West (the present Ontario) caused the bulk of French-Canadians to join hands with Conservatives.[12] The conversion was not to prove permanent. As we shall see in the next chapter, French Canadians were won back to the Liberal party in the eighteen-nineties.

By the eighteen-seventies, then, the distinction between the political behaviour of Catholics in continental Europe, and those in the Anglo-American world, had opened up. In both groups of countries, Catholics were near the open end of the spectrum. Closed Catholicism was nowhere more than in infancy, but Catholics in the two groups of countries were developing different kinds of open Catholicism. In continental Europe, they were involved in an open Catholicism of the right; in Anglo-America, they were involved in an open Catholicism of the left. In the next chapter, it will be shown how one of these open Catholicisms evolved into a closed Catholicism, while the other did not.

3

Variations over time: The development of closed Catholicism c. 1870–1920

During the period covered by this chapter, the conditions for mass political activity were rapidly developing, both in continental Europe and in the Anglo-American world. Towns were growing rapidly – partly because of an overall increase in the population, partly because of an influx from the countryside. This was important, because mass organisation is easier in urban than in rural areas. Industrialisation was affecting more and more countries: from its early strongholds in Britain, Belgium and northern France, it spread outwards until, by the early twentieth century, nearly all the countries in question had their industrial regions. This meant that great concentrations of industrial workers were being formed, with common interests that could be harnessed to political organisation. Literacy levels were rising, with the result that it was possible for political leaders to communicate with a larger and larger section of the population. Mass journalism followed the rise of literacy. Standards of living were rising on the whole, with the result that a somewhat larger proportion of the working population had the leisure and resources for political activity. The dips in the trade cycle were sharp enough, and frequent enough, to ensure that workers were not too easily lulled into contentment.

In the constitutional field, too, conditions for political activity were improving. From the late eighteen-sixties, the franchise was widened in one country after another. The parliament of the North German Confederation, set up in 1866, was elected by manhood suffrage, and this practice was taken over by the parliament of the new German Empire – though not by the individual German states – in 1871. In France, the manhood suffrage already existing became more of a reality as administrative pressures lessened under the Third Republic. In Britain, the franchise was widened in two stages, 1867 and 1884, so that by the latter date virtually all male heads of household, regardless of income, had the vote. Several European countries introduced manhood suffrage by stages: Italy in 1882 and 1912; Belgium in 1893 and 1918; the Netherlands in 1887, 1896 and 1917; Austria in 1896 and 1907. By the end of the period covered in this chapter, the vote was being extended to women. Universal suffrage for male and female was introduced in the United States, Canada, Australia, New Zealand, the Weimar Republic, the Netherlands, Austria, and the Irish Free State. The vote was extended to certain categories of women in Britain, France and Belgium. One of the last strongholds of a restricted franchise – the state of Prussia – passed in 1918–20 to universal suffrage.

Together with extensions of the franchise came greater concern for the secrecy of the vote. In the Anglo-American world, secret ballot was introduced in South Australia in 1858, and spread to most countries, states and provinces by the late eighteen-eighties. In continental Europe, it was introduced in the North German Confederation in 1866 and was carried over into imperial Germany (though not into the elections for individual states). It was introduced in Belgium in 1877 and Italy in 1882. It became compulsory instead of optional in Switzerland in 1872 and France in 1908. These changes were important, because they enabled the masses to make freer use of their electoral rights. The vote by itself was not worth much if the powerful could see how individual electors used it and impose sanctions on those who voted against their wishes. The vote protected by secrecy could make an appreciable difference to the balance of power between social groups.

Not surprisingly, then, the late nineteenth century was the great age of mass mobilisation in most of the countries under consideration. In Britain, the Liberal and Conservative parties developed their mass structure from the late eighteen-sixties. In Germany, the Centre party and the Social Democrats were doing the same by the Eighteen-nineties. In Belgium, Catholics, Socialists and Liberals were doing so from the eighteen-eighties. Even in the Australasian colonies, where the smallness of the population for long made party organisation superfluous, organised parties were appearing by the eighteen-nineties. By 1920, all the countries under consideration had to varying extents developed mass parties.

The same was happening with social organisations. The late nineteenth century was the springtime of the trade-union movement. In 1870, no country – not even Britain – had a trade-union movement which embraced more than a small part of the labour force. In the following decades, various pressures combined to secure an explosion of trade-union membership. Legal restraints which had hampered the development of trade unions in many countries were removed – for instance in France in 1884 and Germany in 1890. Increasing prosperity made organisation easier among skilled workers and – more striking still – made its extension possible to the unskilled. Middle-class socialist intellectuals provided an ideology which over much of Europe gave labour leaders a goal and a rationale. By 1920, trade unionism was a mass movement in all the more industrialised countries of the world.

Other social organisations developed in the same way, if less spectacularly. The co-operative movement was much more widespread in 1920 than it had been in 1870. Farmers' organisations had by the early twentieth century become major pressure groups in Germany, the Low Countries, North America and Australasia, and to some extent elsewhere. Friendly societies were given a powerful boost when, in the late nineteenth and early twentieth centuries, state insurance schemes in many countries built upon them. Youth movements, adult education movements, employers' organisations – all these developed during the same period.

These changes meant that the pre-conditions for the growth of a closed Catholicism at last existed. In continental Europe, the opportunities were taken. Catholics, like other groups, built up their parties and social organisations.

At the outset of this period, the only country with an effective Catholic party – as distinct from a conservative alliance in which Catholics took part – was Germany. The Centre party, launched at the end of 1870 as the *de facto* political organ of German Catholics, quickly found itself playing a more crucial role than its leaders had anticipated; for almost at once, a quarrel, known to history as the *Kulturkampf,* blew up between Chancellor Bismarck and the Catholic Church. It arose from a series of misunderstandings, rather than from set policy on either side, but was none the less bitter for that. Catholics were provoked by the state's support for Italian unity, and for the protection it gave to Catholic opponents of the doctrine of papal infallibility in the education system. Bismarck on his side objected to the formation of a confessional bloc within the newly-created German Empire, whose unity was still so fragile. He decided that the Church must be brought under stricter control, and between 1871 and 1875 a series of important changes were made in Church-state relations. The details of the legislation vary between one part of Germany and another, for many issues were matters for state rather than imperial legislation, and not all German states were embroiled to the same extent. Roughly speaking, one can say that Catholic schools were brought under stricter state control; many religious orders were banished from part or all of Germany; bishops' powers to discipline their clergy were restricted; the training of clerical students was put under state control; and civil marriage was made obligatory. Priests and bishops who resisted were jailed, banished, or deprived of their stipends; and diplomatic relations with the Vatican were broken.

Among German Catholics, this onslaught aroused a surge of solidarity. At the general election of 1871 – before the *Kulturkampf* had got under way – the Centre party gained seventeen per cent of the vote and sixty-one seats. In the general election of 1874, at the height of the struggle, it gained twenty-eight per cent of the vote and ninety-one seats. Analysis of these results indicates that it must have gained the support of virtually every German-speaking practising Catholic – a rate of mobilisation that was not achieved by Catholics in most parts of Europe till much later, if at all.[1] While the Centre party never quite repeated the success of 1874, it remained a major party in German politics through the period covered by this chapter and beyond. Bismarck soon found it prudent to compose his quarrel with the Catholic

Church; and from 1890 till the advent of Hitler in 1933, the Centre was generally part of the governing coalition in Germany.

Developments in Germany were imitated, with varying degrees of rapidity, in other continental countries. In Belgium, the loose and diffuse Conservative and Catholic organisations seemed in the early seventies to be even more disorganised than before: the emergence of an ultramontane group, which wanted to reconstruct Belgian society on the lines of the *Syllabus of Errors* and which was regarded with dismay by more moderate Catholics, led to acrimonious intra-Catholic controversy. However, the divided Catholics were shocked into unity by the militant Liberal government of 1878–84. This administration abolished financial aid to Catholic schools, ended religious instruction in state schools, and broke off diplomatic relations with the Vatican. Catholics countered by developing a mass political organisation, and at the general election of 1884 won a decisive victory. The Catholic party remained in power for thirty years, winning election after election, and agreeing to share power in 1914 not because of electoral defeat but because foreign invasion made national unity a patriotic duty. During this period, it survived unscathed a sweeping extension of the franchise (1893) and the adoption of proportional representation (1899). It also composed serious internal disputes on defence, social and colonial policy. Its only splinter group, a left-wing party led by a Flemish priest called Adolf Daens, never won more than two seats. If the German Centre party was impressive for the volume of support it could call out in a moment of crisis, the Belgian Catholic party was impressive for its durability.

In the Netherlands, developments followed some way behind those in Belgium. During the seventies, the Catholic-Liberal alliance (which, as we saw in the last chapter, was already on the point of dissolution) finally broke down. The points at issue were curiously similar to those in Belgium: the refusal by a Liberal government to maintain diplomatic representation in Rome and its introduction of a school law loaded against denominational schools. The reaction of Dutch Catholics could not, however, be identical with that of their

Belgian neighbours, for they were only a minority: they could not defeat the Liberals without allies. The Conservative party was not a practicable partner: it was by tradition anti-Catholic, and anyway in decline. There was, however, another group in the Dutch parliament: the Anti-Revolutionaries, representatives of popular Calvinism. In ideology these were probably the most anti-Catholic group of all, but they had one thing in common with Catholics: they disliked the Liberals' hostility to denominational schools. Their leader, Abraham Kuyper, saw the necessity of an alliance between Catholic and Anti-Revolutionary if the Liberal school legislation was to be reversed, and set to work to achieve it. The Catholics were diffident at first, but by the eighties most of them had come round to his way of thinking, and in 1888 the first coalition government of Catholics and Anti-Revolutionaries came to power. The cohesion of the Catholic group must not be exaggerated. It was divided into conservative and progressive wings, with little party discipline. None the less, with its Protestant partners it held office for over forty per cent of the time between 1888 and 1920. Its strength in parliament was maintained at a steady twenty-five per cent of the seats, which made it sometimes the largest party in the house.

The Swiss experience combined elements of the German, Belgian and Dutch developments. Switzerland had a *Kulturkampf* of its own in the eighteen-seventies, when a number of measures hostile to the Catholic Church were implemented, and a constitutional revision was forced through which largely divided the country on Protestant-Catholic lines. This ended any attempt to maintain the Conservatives as an interconfessional party: thenceforward they were a *de facto* Catholic party, and conservative Protestants maintained an organisation of their own. However, Catholics maintained a power base in those cantons where they had a majority; and by the end of the century the rise of socialism helped to bring about a *rapprochement* between them and their erstwhile Radical enemies. From 1891, the Conservative party had one representative in the seven-man Swiss government; from 1919, it had two. At cantonal level, by 1912 it controlled the government in nine cantons and half-cantons, and was an important minority in six.[2] As in Germany, Catholics had passed from being an isolated opposition to being part of the 'establishment'.

Somewhat similar developments occurred in Austria. From 1879, Austria was generally governed by a conservative coalition of Slavs and clerically-minded Germans, but differences of nationality were always too acute for any kind of unified party to emerge. Even on a religious basis, such a party proved impossible: attempts by Cardinal Rauscher of Vienna to found one failed, and the Christian Social parties which emerged during the nineties among Poles, Czechs, Slovenes and Italians proved as nationalistic as their non-clerical counterparts.[3] Within the German-speaking ethnic group, however, Catholic politics developed rapidly. In the seventies, there was a loose, conservative-minded, parliamentary grouping of German clericals. In 1891, however, a Vienna advocate, Karl Lueger, founded a Christian Social party with a tighter organisation and a wider clientele. Lueger's party rapidly expanded, and at the general election of 1907 – the first held under manhood suffrage – it became the largest single party in the Austrian parliament. It remained a major party in the truncated post-1918 Austria.

A Catholic party was particularly slow to emerge in Italy. The reason can be found in the policy of boycotting parliamentary elections which the Vatican imposed on Italian Catholics for well over thirty years after the fall of Rome in 1870. The policy was only slowly modified in face of the rising tide of socialism during the opening years of the twentieth century. A papal encyclical of 1905, *Il fermo proposito,* authorised Catholics to vote in those constituencies where the bishop of the diocese deemed it advisable. As a result of this relaxation, sixteen deputies classified as 'Catholics' were elected in 1905 and twenty in 1913. However, the Vatican made clear that they could not be considered spokesmen for Catholic interests, and they did not form a united party. Rather they owed their election to local pacts with Liberals, and many Liberals also owed their election to Catholic support. Thus, the pattern developing under papal auspices in pre-war Italy resembled the open Catholicism of a previous generation, rather than the closed Catholicism which was becoming usual in other continental countries. Catholics tended to be part of a wide-ranging political coalition, rather than developing a party of their own.

However, even in Italy, a Catholic-inspired party emerged at last. The change came after the war. The introduction of manhood suffrage meant that a new electorate was ready to be captured. Pope Benedict XV (1914–22) was less unfriendly to the idea of a Catholic party than his predecessors Leo XIII (1878–1903) or Pius X (1903–14). Accordingly a new grouping, the Italian Popular party, was launched in 1919. It was formally non-confessional, but its programme was Catholic in inspiration, and among its leaders were many who had been active in various Catholic organisations. At the first post-war general election in 1919, it won twenty per cent of the vote. The figures show that the party had not mobilised all the practising Catholics in Italy – whatever their proportion of the male population might be, it was certainly higher than twenty per cent – and one can deduce that many Catholics still preferred the Liberal option. For a new party, however, the results were promising.

The one continental country where it proved impossible to develop an effective Catholic party was France. This was not for lack of cause: anti-clericalism went further in France than in any other country examined in this book. There were two waves of anti-clerical legislation, the first in the eighteen-eighties, the second between 1900 and 1905. When they were over, Catholic schools had been deprived of all state aid; most religious orders had been expelled; Church property had been taken over by the state; government stipends to the clergy had been abolished; diplomatic relations with the Vatican had been broken, and Church and state formally separated. In return, the Church received the freedom to conduct its affairs without state interference, and in the long run this was probably a blessing; but at the time, most French Catholics felt bitterly resentful.

Yet attempts to form a French Catholic party repeatedly failed. Not only were French Catholics divided into left and right – that was true in every other continental country – but they were also riven by a cleavage peculiar to France: a disagreement over the nature of the state. Some were prepared to accept the Third Republic, but others would be content with nothing less than a return to monarchy. It was on this obstacle that attempts to build unity repeatedly foundered. In 1885, a noted Catholic politician, Count Albert de Mun, proposed to form a Catholic party, but Leo XIII discouraged him because he feared that such a party would be too monarchist. In the eighteen-nineties, Leo's alternative became clear, when he urged Catholics to rally to the republic. This meant, in effect, allying with moderate republicans – in other words, the pope was urging on his French flock a form of open Catholicism. His policy antagonised many Catholic monarchists without in the long run conciliating non-Catholic republicans. When the Dreyfus affair erupted in 1899, the line between clerical and anticlerical hardened again; and Catholics, still divided amongst themselves, were forced back into isolation. A somewhat more successful attempt at a Catholic party, the *Action libérale populaire,* existed from 1901 to 1919, but it accepted the republic and so gained no support from monarchists. Thus the pattern of an earlier age survived for an exceptionally long time in France. While Catholics generally voted for one or other conservative faction, the conservatives were not a party but a loose grouping of divergent forces, not all of them sympathetic to Catholicism. This loosely-structured situation survived the First World War. At the first post-war election in 1919, the only new feature was that the conservative forces, allied in the *Bloc national,* were able, thanks to exceptional divisions among their opponents, momentarily to achieve what had eluded them since the eighteen-seventies – a parliamentary majority.

In another way, too, closed Catholicism was developing in continental Europe: Catholic social organisations were burgeoning. By the eighteen-seventies, paternally-minded upper- and middle-class Catholics were paying increasing attention to the growing class of industrial workers. Welfare organisations of various kinds proliferated in all the continental countries under discussion in this book. To increasingly class-conscious workers, however, paternalism was not enough, and in the eighteen-nineties Catholic trades unionism took off almost simultaneously in several countries.

The importance of these unions must not be exaggerated. Figures assembled by Michael Fogarty for the period about 1920 suggest that among manual workers socialist trade unionists outnumbered Christian ones by six to one in Germany, five to one in Austria, eleven to one in Belgium, overwhelmingly in France, and by smaller proportions in Italy and the Netherlands.[4] However, as much of the manual working class seems already to have been lost to the Church, the proportion of practising Catholic workers who rallied to the Christian trade unions may have been higher.

Catholics in other social groups, too, were developing their own organisations. French Catholic employers had their own associations from 1884; the Dutch were beginning to imitate them from 1907, and the Belgians from the end of the First World War. Youth movements of various kinds developed in the late nineteenth century, especially in Italy and France; while in Germany, Austria, Switzerland and the Netherlands, the Kolping associations (mentioned in the last chapter) remained influential. Farmers' organisations of one kind or another were developed in Germany, Italy, France, Belgium and the Netherlands. The *Boerenbond* in Flanders, which organised Flemish farmers into a vast network of co-operative, educational and marketing activities, was particularly influential. Finally, in some countries all-class mutual benefit organisations were being developed. The best-known was the German *Volksverein,* founded in 1890; it was imitated in Switzerland in 1904 and Austria in 1909. The Italian *Opera dei congressi,* founded in 1868, was even more wide-ranging. By 1904, it comprised 2432 organisations – mutual aid societies, producer and consumer co-operatives, workers' societies, farmers' societies, rural loan banks, and so on.[5]

With increasing proliferation came increasing differentiation. During this period, two kinds of social organisation emerged, which can be labelled the **interest group** and the **ginger group.** To take an example: the interest group for employers is a trade association. It looks after every aspect of its members' welfare, representing them in negotiations with other interest groups and with the state, and perhaps carrying out recreational and educational functions as well. Ginger groups in this field are societies which seek to inject the larger interest group with their specific philosophy, whether it be Catholic, evangelical Protestant, socialist, or other. Fogarty has used a similar distinction in the labour field, where he talks of trade unions (equivalent of my interest group) and workers' leagues (equivalent of my ginger group); but the distinction can be employed for employers', farmers' and other kinds of group.

In the labour field, the Catholics of continental Europe favoured interest-group organisations. Distinct Catholic trade unions were built up in the Netherlands, Belgium, France, Switzerland, Italy and Austria. The only country where Catholics preferred to join in wider groupings was Germany, where, on the whole and with exceptions in particular areas, they developed inter-denominational Christian trade unions with Protestant support. In areas other than labour, however, ginger groups were more common. Most Catholic employers' organisations were ginger groups; only in the Netherlands did an interest group exist. There, the Catholic Federation of Employers' Trade Associations, founded in 1919, represented Catholic employers in negotiations with trade unions and governments, just as its Protestant and neutral counterparts did. In the agricultural world, most specifically Catholic organisations were of the ginger-group type; interest-group Catholic farmers' organisations were confined to the Netherlands and Belgium. However, individual Catholics were prominent in building up the formally neutral farmers' interest groups which existed in other European countries.

The growth of Catholic parties and social organisations in continental Europe was underpinned by the growth of a distinctive Catholic social doctrine. The origins of the quest for a distinctive doctrine went back many decades. From early in the nineteenth century, individual Catholics – such as de Villeneuve-Bargemont in France, Ducpétiaux in Belgium, and Bishop Ketteler in Germany – were concerned at the inequities of the existing social system. Dissatisfied with the prevailing economic doctrine, laissez-faire liberalism, which made such inequities possible, they sought to develop an alternative. In the eighteen-eighties, the search for such an alternative was given added urgency by the rise of socialism.

To most Christians in the late nineteenth century, socialism seemed an enemy: not surprising, since so many socialist leaders, such as Marx, Kropotkin, Bebel, Guesde, showed their own contempt and hostility for Christianity. Yet socialism appealed to the workers because they had real grievances. Denunciation was not enough: an alternative solution to these grievances must be found.

During the eighteen-eighties, two rival schools of Catholic social thought emerged. A conservative school, whose best-known figures were Charles Périn in Belgium and Bishop Freppel of Angers in France, argued that the social problem was primarily a moral one, to be remedied by fostering the Christian virtue of charity. While this school conceded that state intervention might be necessary in particular circumstances, it believed that such intervention must be kept within strict bounds, for fear of being drawn into socialism. A second, more venturesome school, had representatives in France (Albert de Mun, the Marquis de la Tour du Pin) and in Belgium (Mgr Doutreloux), as well as dominating Catholic thought in Germany, Switzerland and Austria. The members of this school denied that the social question was simply a moral issue. They felt that there were injustices in the structure of society which could and should be put right by legislation. They were therefore less wary of state intervention.[6]

The dispute between the two schools was resolved by the publication of Leo XIII's encyclical *Rerum novarum* in 1891. The radicalism of this encyclical can be exaggerated. Its denunciations of socialism were wholehearted enough to satisfy the most conservative, but it acknowledged the necessity for state intervention and thus, on the central issue, came down in favour of the more liberal school of Catholic social thought. This was important for maintaining the impetus towards a closed Catholicism. It meant that Catholics were committed to a social doctrine which differentiated them from some other conservatives, and so made it harder for them to maintain the pan-conservative alliance which had previously been the normal political stance of Catholics in continental Europe.

There was another way, too, in which the development of

Catholic social doctrine was important. It gave rise to a network of congresses, study groups and periodicals. In almost every country one particular congress had particular prestige – the *Katholikentage* of Germany, Austria and Switzerland, the *semaines sociales* of France, the *settimane sociali* of Italy. At these congresses, the leaders of the different Catholic parties and social organisations were often among the star speakers. They met each other, exchanged views, and generated a common body of ideas. The social study conferences acted as the liaison organisations of closed Catholicism.

In yet another way, closed Catholicism was developing in continental Europe during this period: clerical involvement in politics was increasing. In the preceding era, when mass mobilisation had not yet occurred and politics was the preserve of a small elite, Catholic political leadership had often been provided by the aristocracy. But as politics became more democratic, the clergy came more into prominence. This was particularly evident in the building up of social organisations. Priests played an important part in their formation: they provided an infant farmers' or workers' organisation with a leadership which could not easily have been obtained in any other way. An English Quaker student of Belgian agriculture, for instance, noted that 'the great development of agricultural societies is almost entirely the work of the Catholic or Conservative party; and it is doubtful whether it would have been half so important but for the whole-hearted devotion of hundreds of priests, who have made themselves responsible for managing and superintending the little village societies'.[7] The histories of the Catholic social movement are studded with the names of priests who played a leading role in the development of such movements: Fathers Alphonse Ariëns and Henri Poels in the Netherlands, Fathers Franz Hitze and Christoph Moufang in Germany, Cardinal Mermillod in Switzerland, and many others.

Even in the strictly political field, clergy remained prominent during this period. The priest-deputy remained a frequent phenomenon, often appearing on the left of Catholic politics. In France, the *abbés démocrates*, priests of left-wing sympathies of whom the best known was Abbé Lemire of

Hazebrouck, were well-known figures in parliament during the eighteen-nineties. In Belgium, an equivalent figure was Father Adolf Daens, leader of a radical splinter group from the Catholic party.[8] In the Netherlands, the first priest to sit in parliament, Mgr Schaepman, had to fight a long contest with a right-wing faction before uniting the Catholic party under his own leadership. In Italy, the moving spirit of the Popular party was a priest, Don Luigi Sturzo, though he did not himself become a deputy. As usual, priest-deputies were particularly prominent in Germany. The Prussian Landtag had twelve such deputies in 1899 and fourteen in 1912; in the Reichstag the figure reached its highest level, twenty-three in 1903.[9] Alsace-Lorraine signalled its annexation to the German Empire by electing two bishops and five priests among its fifteen deputies.[10]

Clerical activity was not confined to legislatures, but could be important in electioneering. In Belgium, according to the historian who has specialised in the topic, the political activity of the bishops reached its peak in the years 1879–84.[11] This was the period when the bishops believed the Liberal government was attempting to dechristianise the schools, and they called on the electors as a religious duty to oppose them. Priests could also be active in the local organisation of political parties. This seems to have been particularly important in Germany. The Centre party's electoral committee for the district of Sieg in 1898 comprised forty-four clerics and twenty-two laymen. The committee for the district of Geldern was about fifty per cent clerical in the same year.[12] The author of an electoral study of Trier concludes that it was above all the clergy who kept electioneering going for the Centre party.[13] An observer of Bavarian politics wrote that 'the Center had a first-class party organisation. It had the all-powerful backing of the bishops whose mandates to the laity strongly influenced the opinion of the faithful. The clergy constituted an extra-parliamentary propaganda machine, unrivaled in efficiency. The "chaplainocracy" did not hesitate openly to urge the election of Catholic deputies from the pulpits. A vast army of ecclesiastics did their bidding. Party newspapers, often edited by priests, flooded the country.'[14] The American scholar, A. L. Lowell, writing in 1896, classed

Bavaria with Belgium as one of the two parts of Europe in which the clergy took the most active part in politics.[15]

France was another country where the political activity of the clergy was important. Here it was not simply a matter of organisation: the clergy seem to have been exceptionally prone to use their spiritual authority in order to induce the electors to vote in what the clergy considered the right way. There were forty-four cases in France of elections being invalidated on the grounds of undue clerical influence, all of them in the period 1876–1902.[16] This by itself would be an imperfect index of the degree of clerical involvement: election cases were judged by parliament, and since the French parliament in this period had an anti-clerical majority, its decision may not have been free from bias. But even from other sources we hear much of clerical influence during this period. In the general elections of 1876 and 1877, the government (then still Conservative) issued confidential circulars to the bishops asking them to be discreet in their language.[17] A Catholic historian like Daniel-Rops can write of tradesmen in the eighteen-seventies being 'denounced by name from the pulpit as republicans and punished with savage boycott of their goods', or of a preacher in 1902 declaring that at the election there were only two candidates: Jesus and Barabbas.[18]

The extent to which a closed Catholicism developed during the period 1870–1920 should not be exaggerated. Some bishops and clergy, and not least the Vatican, had doubts about how far such a move should be encouraged. The danger was that Catholic political parties and social organisations threw up strong leaders who might show a disconcerting independence. A spectacular example was Leo XIII's brush with the Centre party. In 1887, while Leo XIII was negotiating a *rapprochement* with Bismarck, he asked the Centre party to vote for a military service law which Bismarck had much at heart. However, for policy reasons of its own, the Centre party declined to fall in with this request and made clear that it would dissolve itself if the pope persisted. Leo XIII backed down. In France, Leo XIII deprecated the proposal by Albert de Mun in 1885 to form a Catholic party, and preferred French Catholics to act in coalition with non-

Catholic conservatives. His successor, Pius X, while more friendly to a closed Catholicism in France, was hostile to it in Italy. In 1904 he broke up the *Opera dei congressi,* the powerful movement of Italian Catholic laity, because it was showing independent tendencies. The only pope who was generally favourable to the idea of Catholic parties was Benedict XV (1914–22). It was with his approval, for instance, that the Popular party was launched in Italy.

Even among the lay leaders, there were hesitations about how far it was desirable to emphasise their Catholicism. To allow their organisations to be too closely linked to the Church meant reducing their recruiting base and their independence. Of the *de facto* Catholic parties in continental Europe, only those of Belgium and the Netherlands contained the word 'Catholic' in their title, and only the Austrian party used the term 'Christian'. In Germany, Italy and France, the non-denominational titles of Centre, Popular, and Popular Liberal were deliberately chosen by the party founders. In Switzerland, at the founding conference in 1912 a minority wanted the party to be called 'Catholic', but the decision to call it 'Conservative' was carried by 145 votes to 37.[19] Nor was this preference for a non-denominational title simply a matter of window-dressing. The greatest crisis which the Centre party suffered in this period occurred in 1906–9, when one wing of the party argued that they should more actively recruit non-Catholic members, while another wing sharply disagreed. The quarrel was linked to one in the trade-union movement, between those who felt that Catholics should build up purely Catholic trade unions, and those who favoured inter-denominational unions with Protestant as well as Catholic support. The advocates of openness were more influential and received the sympathy of Rome.

Another brake on the development of closed Catholicism in this period was that it did not appeal to all Catholics equally. Only in a great religious crisis like the *Kulturkampf* would Catholics rally solidly round their leaders. While to a practising Catholic his religion was important, in quiet times it was not the only thing that would influence his vote or his participation in a social organisation. He had class, regional and perhaps ethnic interests to defend as well, and these might affect his choice. A good example can be seen in the history of the Centre party, which after its great success in 1874 never again succeeded in attracting all German Catholics under its banner. To the Catholic aristocracy – which included some of the bishops – it was demagogic and a little vulgar. To Catholic workers, the Social Democrats were a seductive alternative, for they seemed better champions of working-class interests. Polish and Alsatian Catholics maintained their own parties throughout, even during the *Kulturkampf*. According to one shrewd recent analysis, the Centre party was a vehicle for 'the grievances of the Catholic peasantry and lower-middle class' and for 'the aspirations of middle-class Catholics'. [20] Yet even these social groups could not be counted on. There were signs in the eighteen-nineties that Catholic peasants were defecting to agrarian parties, until the Centre shifted its policy to take account of their interests. The difficulties which the Centre faced in retaining its electorate could be paralleled, with necessary changes, in all the other Catholic parties of continental Europe.

None the less, when these qualifications are made, there can be no doubt that the position of Catholics in continental Europe changed dramatically in the period 1870–1920. In 1870, closed Catholicism was in its infancy. There were no denominational parties, except in Germany. There were hardly any Catholic social organisations. By 1920, every country in the region except France had a recognisably Catholic party. Catholic social organisations were numerous and significant. Catholic clergy took an active part in both parties and social organisations, using both their organisational skills and their spiritual authority to further their cause.

What about the Anglo-American world? It would be surprising if Catholics in these countries showed no sign of developing in the same direction as those in continental Europe. After all, the economic and social factors which made a closed Catholicism possible in Europe also operated to a great extent in Anglo-America. And indeed, signs of the emergence of a closed Catholicism can be detected in the Anglo-American world.

One such sign was the development of Catholic social doctrine. English-speaking Catholics made as much of a contribution to this as did those of many continental countries. The English Cardinal Manning (Archbishop of Westminster, 1865–92) is counted as one of the pioneers of Catholic social thought. The American Cardinal Gibbons (Archbishop of Baltimore, 1877–1921) is credited with a decisive intervention in the development of papal social doctrine, when in 1887 he persuaded Rome not to forbid Catholics joining what was then the major American labour organisation. Among the exponents of Catholic social teaching were Cardinal Moran in Australia, Father John A. Ryan and Father Peter Dietz in the United States, Father Lambert McKenna in Ireland. Societies and study groups were set up, such as the Catholic Social Guild (1908) in England, the Leo Guild (1912) in Ireland, the *école sociale populaire* in Montreal.

Another way in which Catholicism seemed to become more closed in several Anglo-American countries was that there, as on the continent, Catholic clergy came to play a more active part in politics. In Australia, Cardinal Moran of Sydney had an important effect on the future of politics by throwing his influence in support of the young Labor party; and Archbishop Mannix of Melbourne played a leading role in the violent conscription controversy of 1916–17. In the United States, Archbishop Ireland of St Paul was a frequent speaker on political issues; he was countered publicly by other bishops and priests who disagreed with his interpretations. Even in Britain, where the small size of the Catholic population might have implied powerlessness, Catholic clergy were not entirely without influence. According to one view, a letter from Cardinal Manning calling on Catholics to oppose candidates who were unsound on the education question was a cause of the Liberals' disappointment in the general election of 1885.[21]

Two areas where clerical influence was particularly important were Ireland and Quebec. In Ireland, the political influence of the clergy seems to have reached its peak at a period slightly earlier than this, about 1850–70,[22] but it remained important for the rest of the nineteenth century. Priests, for instance, were *ex officio* members of the county conventions which selected Nationalist candidates for parliament. In Quebec, the greatest clerical activity occurred in the eighteen-seventies. In the federal elections of 1874 and 1878 and the provincial elections of 1875, there were numerous complaints of clerical intimidation on behalf of Ultramontane candidates. Not all the Quebec bishops approved of this activity, and intervention from Rome eventually led to its moderation, but it remained a force through the eighteen-eighties and beyond.

In one important area the difference between the continental and the Anglo-American countries proved to be insignificant. This was education. A denominational education system could be seen as an important underpinning to a closed Catholicism, because it ensured that Catholics shared an experience which set them apart from the wider society. Catholics in continental countries were not on average more successful in building up denominational education systems than those in the Anglo-American world; in both groups of countries, Catholics in the period covered by this chapter made prodigious efforts to build up such systems. The degree of success varied widely, being largely conditioned by the amount of state aid that Catholics were able to secure. In some countries of both groups, Catholics had relatively complete success – Belgium, the Netherlands, Quebec, Ireland. In other countries of both groups, success was more patchy – France, Italy, the United States, England. The line between relative closedness and relative openness in this field cuts right across the line between closedness and openness in other areas.

In other ways, however, Anglo-American Catholics did not move so far towards the closed end of the spectrum as those of continental Europe. The Catholic trade-union movement, for instance, so substantial on the continent, was insignificant in the Anglo-American world. The examples which I have come across of attempts at forming Catholic trade unions have no more than curiosity value. Some are said to have existed in the British textile industry.[23] Another was founded in Kingstown, Co. Dublin.[24] Bishop Quigley of Buffalo, New York, is said to have attempted to organise Catholic labour unions.[25] Even in Quebec, where Catholic unions were to be important in the subsequent period, they were only just beginning in the period covered by this chapter: the first dated from 1902.[26] The overwhelmingly prevalent pattern in the Anglo-American world was for trade unions to be built up on a non-confessional basis, with Catholics taking their place on an equal footing with others.

The same was true of other social organisations. For instance, the most important rural movement in the Ireland of this period, the Irish Agricultural Organisation Society, was non-confessional, with a Protestant, Sir Horace Plunkett, as its president, and a Jesuit priest, Father Peter Finlay, as its vice-president. Only in Quebec were most of the rural movements of Catholic inspiration. There, the *Syndicat central des agriculteurs du Canada* was given episcopal patronage in the eighteen-nineties. The *Cercles agricoles* were founded by the Abbé Pilote, and the *Comptoir co-opératif de Montréal* was founded under the inspiration of Father Bellemare, S.J.[27]

In so far as Anglo-American Catholics did build up distinct organisations in this period, they were nearly always ginger groups acting within non-confessional parties or unions. In Britain, the Association of Catholic Trade Unionists sought to prevent the Labour party from adopting a form of socialism condemned by the Church. Also in Britain, the Catholic Federation – a non-party pressure group – questioned candidates before the general election of January 1910 on their attitudes to education. In Australia, the Australian Catholic Federation adopted a similar policy in the state elections during 1914–15. A Catholic Federation was active at the same period in New Zealand. In the United States, the American Federation of Catholic Societies (founded 1901) acted as a channel for the expression of Catholic views. Within the American Federation of Labor, Father Dietz founded a group known as the Militia for Christ, to ensure that Catholic social principles were borne in mind. Such bodies fell far short of the highly-developed network of interlocking social organisations which continental Catholics built up.

Nor did Catholic parties develop in the Anglo-American world. The Irish Parliamentary party behaved in some respects as the representative in the British parliament of Catholic interests; but, as was shown in Chapter 1, it was anxious to stress that it was a national and not a Catholic party. Elsewhere, the possibility of a Catholic party was occasionally broached. In Australia, Archbishop Mannix of Melbourne threatened the Labor party in 1915 that, if it did not pay more attention to Catholic demands in education, a Catholic party might be started. In the United States, the idea of a closed Catholicism had particular attractions for German Catholics. Aware of the achievements of the Centre party in their country of origin and more dubious than Irish Catholics about the virtues of American civilisation, they explored the possibility of forming Catholic workers' organisations and even more distantly of a Catholic party.[28] A more serious potential for a Catholic party existed in Canada during the eighteen-seventies, when a wing of the Conservative party, calling itself the Ultramontanes, campaigned on a platform entitled *le programme catholique*. However, the Ultramontanes never became an entirely distinct party. Moreover, they were discountenanced by a portion of the hierarchy and eventually by Rome, and during the eighteen-eighties lapsed into ineffectiveness.

On the whole, Catholics in the Anglo-American countries found a place for themselves within the existing or emerging party structures. In the United States, the pattern persisted whereby Catholics tended to form part of the coalition supporting the Democratic party. Where deviations from the pattern occurred, it was not because Catholics set up a party of their own, but because Republicans made raids, more or less successful, on the Democratic vote. In the eighteen-eighties, some Republicans sought to woo the Irish-Americans. The results were not promising, and in the eighteen-nineties they preferred to court the non-Irish ethnic groups, whom they hoped might be resentful of Irish hegemony in Catholic political life.[29] Again their success was limited.

In the Australian colonies (federated into the Commonwealth of Australia in 1900) a somewhat similar situation eventually emerged. The shifting groups which were all that the Australian colonies had had in the way of a party system began in the eighteen-eighties to settle down into more organised parties. By the time of federation, the Australian Labor party had emerged as a major force. Over the following twenty years, the Catholic vote became increasingly identified with Labor. The process had its ups and downs, for some Labor men were militant secularists, and on education the Labor party was no nearer the Catholic position than were the other parties. Indeed, if a split on the conscription issue in 1916–17 had not driven many of the English-descended members out of the party, it might never have become as popular with the Catholic electorate as it eventually did. However, by about 1920 the identification of Catholic and Labor was marked.

In New Zealand, the process was slower, and the preference of Catholic voters for the Labour party did not reach its full development till after the period covered by this chapter. The Liberal and Conservative (later Reform) parties were still the major parties around 1920, with Labour only in third place. Not much is known about Catholic political behaviour in this period, but there are indications that Catholics were already attracted by the Labour party, as they were in Australia.[30] The attraction, however, may have been less complete. The Reform party had an active no-popery wing and a leader, W. F. Massey, of Ulster Protestant origin; on the other hand, the Liberals had a Catholic, Sir Joseph Ward, as their leader for much of the period. There are signs, therefore, that Catholics in New Zealand could differentiate more clearly between non-Labour parties than in Australia, and that they favoured the Liberals.[31] What is beyond question is that here, as in Australia, there was no sign of a specifically Catholic party during the period covered by this chapter.

In Britain, Catholics' choice of which major party to support was not always clear-cut. Conservatives probably had the edge among better-off Catholics and those of native English or Scottish stock – partly on class grounds, partly because on education they were more sympathetic to Catholic schools. But the Liberals were from 1886 committed to home rule for Ireland, and this gave them the advantage among Catholics of Irish birth or descent. Since the latter made up the bulk of the Catholic electorate, it seems fair to conclude that the Catholic vote was disproportionately Liberal during most of the period covered by this chapter. Towards the end,

Labour was emerging as a major party. As in Australia and New Zealand, it had considerable attractions for Catholic electors, who were largely working class. The fact that, like the Liberals, it supported home rule increased those attractions.[32]

In Ireland, the overwhelming majority of Catholics supported the Irish Nationalist party almost to the end of this period. In the final years a new party, Sinn Fein, even more intransigent than the Nationalists, had a meteoric rise. At the general election of 1918, Sinn Fein swept the board in the Catholic parts of Ireland, winning seventy-three seats to the Nationalists' six. In this contest between two competitors for the Catholic vote, the Church formally remained neutral. Individual priests were to be found campaigning for both sides.

The most complex case was Canada. At the outset of this period, French Canadians tended to support the Conservatives. However, from the mid-eighties the Liberal party gained ground among them, not because it was the more Catholic of the two parties, but because its attitude in a series of issues suggested that it was the better defender of French-Canadian interests. Finally, in the federal elections of 1896, the Liberals gained a landslide victory in the province of Quebec, winning forty-nine seats out of sixty-five. Quebec has remained a Liberal stronghold at almost every election since. There are indications that in English-speaking Canada the Catholic minority had all along favoured the Liberals, for the Conservative party tended to discredit itself in Catholic eyes by attracting a no-popery fringe. Thus, Canadian Catholics came to match the pattern found in the rest of the Anglo-American world. Instead of seeking to form their own political party, they found a niche for themselves within the nationwide, catch-all parties.

It was in the period covered by this chapter, then that the distinction opened up between continental Europe on the one hand and the Anglo-American countries on the other. True, the distinction can be exaggerated: it was one of pace rather than of direction. In both groups of countries, movement occurred from the open end of the spectrum towards the closed end; but the movement was limited and hesitant in the Anglo-American world; it was considerably more vigorous in continental Europe.

The next question that arises is: why should this divergence have occurred? Part of the reason may be found in the different outlook of the labour movement in the two groups of countries. In continental Europe, trade unions were often built up by committed socialists who included the churches, alongside the aristocracy and the bourgeoisie, among their targets for condemnation. In the Anglo-American world, on the other hand, some labour leaders were committed Christians, while only a minority were militantly anti-Christian. Various reasons can be suggested for this contrast. It is possible that social mobility was, on the whole, greater in the Anglo-American world than in continental Europe, and that working-class leaders were, therefore, less likely to judge the system as wholly unfair to them. In Britain at least, the trade-union movement had a long history and had already established a tradition not unfriendly to organised religion, before atheistic socialism became an intellectual fashion. Whatever the causes, there is no doubt about the importance of this divergence. It meant that in the Anglo-American world, working-class Catholics could participate without discomfort – and without alarming their clergy – in a unified trade-union movement. Indeed in the United States at the beginning of the twentieth century, it was estimated that about one-half of those in trade unions were Catholic.[33] In continental Europe, on the other hand, working-class Catholics faced a labour movement which scorned their religion as superstitious. This alienated the more pious among them; it also antagonised their clergy. A major reason for the development of Christian trade unions on the continent was to protect religiously-inclined workers from contamination by socialism.

The same contrast existed in the political wing of the labour movement. Social Democratic parties on the continent were often built up by anti-religious militants. The German party, for instance – the largest and most successful of them all – at one stage tried to induce its members to cut their formal links with the Protestant or Catholic churches, and declare themselves openly as unbelievers. In the Anglo-American world, on the other hand, these problems did not arise. The United States did not even have a socialist party of any importance; neither did Canada until after the period covered by this chapter. Australia, New Zealand and Great Britain did produce Labour parties, but many of the early leaders were Christians of various Protestant traditions, and Catholics had no great difficulty in working with them. Indeed in Australia (1905) and England (1918), the bishops facilitated the movement of Catholics into the labour parties by declaring that the kind of socialism which those parties advocated was not the kind condemned by the Church.

Yet it would be wrong to put too much stress on the divergent character of the labour movement in the two groups of countries. Though the difference undoubtedly reinforced the contrast between closed Catholicism on the continent and open Catholicism in the Anglo-American world, it did not begin it. The divergence was already growing before socialism became a significant force. The Centre party in Germany was a major party while the socialists were still a struggling minority. The Catholic parties in Belgium, Switzerland and the Netherlands had origins going back to well before the beginning of the socialist movements. In Italy, where papal policy forbade the building up of a Catholic party, the energies of zealous Catholics went into building up social organisations, the *Opera dei congressi*, which were flourishing while the socialist movement was still in its infancy. Even in France and Austria, the rise of closed Catholicism occurred at least as early as the rise of closed socialism.

Indeed it would be more accurate to see the rise of closed Catholicism and the rise of socialism as parallel responses to the same development – the increasing mass mobilisation in continental Europe. The two movements even had parallel names. The socialist movement in the late nineteenth century was generally known as Social Democracy. The new developments within Catholicism came by the eighteen-nineties to be known as Christian Democracy. Social Democracy and Christian Democracy were contemporaries, one arising out of the liberal camp and the other out of the conservative.

The origins of the divergence between Catholic political

behaviour in continental Europe and that in the Anglo-American world must, then, be put one stage further back. The crucial factor seems to have been the political alliances made by Catholics in the period roughly 1850 to 1870.

In continental Europe, as was shown in the last chapter, the fifties and sixties saw a drift by Catholics into a conservative alliance. The liberal Catholics, who had been quite influential in preceding decades, found their position increasingly untenable and ceased to be a significant force. No sooner had this concentration of Catholics on the right occurred, than it began to run up against difficulties. The main one was that this position was electorally unsatisfactory. The eighteen-seventies saw liberalism triumph in all the countries of continental Europe. It was already the dominant force in the Netherlands, Switzerland and Italy. It became the strongest force – though divided between three parties – in the new German Empire. In Austria, it was in the ascendant between 1868 and 1879. In France, the Conservative majority in the opening years of the French Republic was overthrown in the general election of 1877, never to be reconstructed, except fleetingly, until after the Second World War. Belgium was the country where the contest was most evenly drawn. There the Catholics regained power in 1870, after thirteen years of Liberal rule. But in 1878 after overhauling their electoral machine, the Liberals won a landslide victory and for the next six years maintained one of the most anti-clerical regimes in Europe.

The liberal hegemony was of short duration in most of these countries. However, while it lasted, it forced Catholics in all of them to rethink their strategy. Some remained loyal to the old pan-conservative coalition, hoping that eventually the tide would turn in their favour; others were not content to stand by methods which had proved electorally injurious. The drawback to the Conservative coalition was that it connected Catholics with unpopular allies – aristocrats, landlords, the propertied classes in general. Small wonder that Catholics began to distance themselves from such allies and organise themselves on a more democratic, but also more purely confessional basis.

This pattern can be seen with varying degrees of clarity in

all the countries of continental Europe. The rise of Catholic parties which was detailed earlier in this chapter in every case involved a shift to the left. In Germany, the Centre party in due course developed a mass organisation which rivalled that of the Social Democrats. In the Netherlands, Mgr Schaepman's success in organising a formal Catholic party at the beginning of the twentieth century represented a defeat for the conservatives in Catholic politics. In Austria, Karl Lueger's Christian Social party was built up in conscious reaction against the aristocratic leadership of the old Conservative party. In Italy, where papal policy prevented the emergence of a Catholic party till the very end of this period, the *Opera dei congressi* was the vehicle of the new, relatively radical, but also more strongly confessional forces. In France, the cleavage between monarchist and republican Catholics was in part a class cleavage, and the gradual advance of republicans at the expense of monarchists was also an advance of democrats at the expense of aristocrats.

The process whereby a closed Catholicism emerged in conscious rejection of conservative allies has been examined with particular clarity for two countries. In Belgium, Karel van Isacker has examined the transformation of the Catholic party in the period 1863–84.[34] He has shown how the party in this period both democratised itself and made itself more strictly confessional. The parliamentarians of the sixties preferred the label 'Conservative' to that of 'Catholic', but the militants of the seventies and eighties insisted on the title 'Catholic'. Their view prevailed, and in the general election of 1884 they led the party to the victory which heralded thirty years of Catholic party rule.

In Switzerland, Urs Altermatt has examined the development of closed Catholicism.[35] He distinguishes between two types of Swiss Catholic – the Stammland and the Diaspora. The Stammlanders were the inhabitants of the traditionally Catholic cantons of Switzerland. They were politically conservative; they emphasised cantonal rights; and – since they were anxious to work with like-minded politicians in Protestant cantons – they laid little stress on their Catholicism. The Diaspora were Catholics living in traditionally Protestant cantons, such as Zurich. They were often recent immigrants and relatively poor. They were politically more radical than the Stammlanders and also more confessional: they cared nothing for alliance with conservative Protestants. As Altermatt tells it, the story of Swiss Catholic politics from about 1880 to the First World War is the story of the contest between these two forces, with the Diaspora slowly getting the upper hand, until in 1912 a political party was formed largely on the lines which they preferred.

In the Anglo-American countries, on the other hand, such calculations did not apply. Far from having to disentangle themselves from a conservative alliance which had proved unprofitable, Anglo-American Catholics committed themselves with increasing clarity during this period to a liberal alliance. In all the Anglo-American countries, they came to commit themselves to the more left-wing of the major parties: Democrats in the United States, Liberals in Canada, Labor in Australia, Liberals and then Labour in Britain and New Zealand. The Irish Parliamentary Party, which Irish Catholics almost solidly supported, was allied to the Liberals in the British parliament. Now these allegiances did not on the whole prove electorally unprofitable. True, in the United Kingdom the Liberal party was in opposition more often than in office after 1886, but it did have periods of office in 1892–5 and 1906–15. In Australia and New Zealand, the young Labour parties to which many Catholics gravitated soon proved electorally successful. In the United States, the Democratic party was not often in a majority nationally, but it usually controlled the states and cities where Catholics were most numerous – and, in a polity so decentralised as the United States then was, this was what mattered. In Canada, the Liberals have been the normal majority party ever since 1896.

Thus the crucial factor in explaining the divergence between Catholics in continental Europe and those in Anglo-America which emerged after 1870 seems to be the nature of the alliances which each had developed during the preceding period. Catholics in continental Europe had become entangled in a conservative alliance which proved electorally damaging. The way out was to move to the left in policy, but also to emphasise Catholicism as a focus of unity. Thus closed

Catholicism developed as an escape route from conservatism. Catholics in the Anglo-American countries, on the other hand, were not under the same pressures. Though some movement towards a closed Catholicism occurred even in those countries, the motivation for it was not nearly so impelling. Anglo-American Catholics developed alliances with the more liberal forces in their respective countries. These alliances proved profitable and were retained.

4

Variations over time: The peak period of closed Catholicism, c. 1920–60

The title of this chapter, the peak period of closed Catholicism, is a simplification. Though true as a global description of these decades, it conceals dips and peaks in the graph. The forces making for a closed Catholicism only just prevailed over, and indeed on occasions failed to prevail over, the forces making for an open Catholicism.

In continental Europe, closed Catholicism in the nineteen-twenties and thirties appeared to be on the decline. Several parties of Catholic inspiration were closed down by Fascist regimes: the Italian Popular party in 1925, the German Centre party in 1933, the Austrian Christian Social party in 1934. In Belgium, the fortunes of the Catholic party fell to their lowest point in the general election of 1936, when defections to Fascists and Flemish nationalists reduced its proportion of the vote to twenty-eight per cent. In France, a party of Catholic inspiration, the *Parti démocrate populaire,* had only limited success, never winning more than twenty-one seats in a house of nearly six hundred. Only in the Netherlands and Switzerland did parties appealing to the Catholic electorate do well. Profiting from the introduction of proportional representation, the Roman Catholic State party in the Netherlands, and the Conservative People's party in Switzerland, produced their best results yet, averaging thirty per cent and twenty-three per cent of the seats in their respective parliaments during the period 1920–40.[1]

Parallel difficulties faced Catholic social organisations in continental Europe. In Italy, Germany and Austria, they were wound up by Fascist regimes. Even where this did not happen, they were damaged, like most other social organisations, by the great depression, and numbers declined.

Perhaps the only relative success was scored by the Catholic trade unions of Belgium, which, while remaining behind the socialist trade unions in strength, managed at least to narrow the gap, from 5:1 in favour of the socialist in 1919, to only 3:2 in 1939.[2]

As far as clerical involvement in politics was concerned, the nineteen-twenties produced a late flowering. Never before – or at least not since the *ancien régime* – were so many clerics in high political positions. The chancellor of Austria was Mgr Seipel. The chairman of the Dutch Catholic parliamentary party was Mgr Nolens. The secretary of the Italian Popular party, until he resigned under pressure from the Vatican in 1923, was Father Luigi Sturzo. Political prelates were particularly thick on the ground in Germany, where Mgr Kaas was chairman of the Centre's parliamentary party, Father Brauns was a long-serving labour minister, Mgr Lauscher was leader of the Centre in the Prussian parliament, and Mgr Leicht was chairman in the Reichstag of the Bavarian People's party, an offshoot from the Centre.

However, as these figures dropped out of politics, no clerical politicians of comparable stature emerged to succeed them. In Germany, hitherto the special home of the priest-deputy, this was the result of a conscious decision. The concordat of 1933 laid down that priests were not to be members of political organisations, a restriction which the Church has on the whole continued to observe since the war. In Austria, too, the hierarchy decided in 1934 to withdraw all clergy from political office, and retained this ban after the war. Elsewhere, the decline of the clerical politician may have been the result of natural evolution. As an increasing proportion of the Catholic population received education, and as the network of social organisations became better established, so it became easier to find lay leaders. Sometimes, too, errors made by clerical leadership could result in a prudent withdrawal from the arena. In Belgium, for instance, after the great depression involved the *Boerenbond* in financial disaster, priests took a less prominent part in its central committee.[3]

There were several reasons for the decline of closed Catholicism during the inter-war years. The pre-war bitterness between clerical and anti-clerical was in most countries dying down. The issues over which they had once fought had generally been settled, one way or another. The restoration of the pope's temporal power had long since ceased to be a cause for which Catholic voters could be mobilised. The question of state aid for the Catholic Church no longer aroused much controversy, either in countries like France, where that aid had been withdrawn, or in countries like Belgium and Italy, where it remained. Even the question of state assistance for Catholic schools aroused fewer passions than previously. Everywhere some kind of settlement had been reached, and though the settlements varied widely between one country and another in their attractiveness for Catholics, almost everywhere they were accepted, with resignation if not with enthusiasm. Even in France, where the settlement had been least satisfactory for the Church, attempts to mobilise Catholics to demand more state aid for their schools aroused little enthusiasm.[4] The reduced saliency of Church-related issues can be verified by anyone who compares the standard histories of Europe in the period 1870–1914 with those of Europe between the wars. In the former, Church-state relations supply a major theme; in the latter, they are scarcely mentioned.

Another factor working in the same direction was the common experience of suffering in the First World War. Most of Europe was involved in the war: Belgium, France, Italy, Austria and Germany. In all these countries, Catholic and Protestant, clerical and anti-clerical were mobilised together and faced the same hardships and dangers. The effect seems to have been most marked where bitterness had previously been greatest, in France. It had been a grievance of French Catholics that the clergy were liable for military service on the same terms as other men, without regard for their sacred character: a law which led to the mobilisation of nearly 25,000 priests, religious and seminarians, and to the death on active service of 4,608 priests.[5] But at least this law ensured that French priests faced suffering and death on the same terms as their lay fellow-citizens, unsheltered by privilege. Many anti-clericals got to know priests for the first time during their common military service, and the result was an increased respect and understanding on both sides. After the war, there was only one attempt to revive the anti-clerical feeling which had previously been so strong in France. It occurred after the general election of 1924 had returned a left-wing majority to Parliament. The prime minister, Édouard Herriot, launched a programme which included several items unpalatable to Catholics, notably the extension to the recovered territories of Alsace-Lorraine of the secular school system which had been built up elsewhere in France. The campaign aroused surprisingly little enthusiasm even among those who were by tradition anti-clerical and was abandoned before it attained its objects.

The most important factor working to erode closed Catholicism during the inter-war period was the rise of fascism, for fascism divided the Catholic camp. Its deification of the state ran contrary to Catholic doctrine and alienated many Catholics. Its advance was a threat to the interests and affections of the many Catholics who had spent their lives building up Catholic parties and Catholic social organisations. On the other hand, its corporatist ideology had affinities, at least on the surface, with the social teaching (to be discussed below) elaborated by the Church in this period. And many of the sentiments to which fascism appealed – nationalism, solidarity, a longing for order, a desire for scapegoats – were as attractive to Catholics as to other citizens.

The degree to which fascism appealed to Catholics varied sharply with the country. It was most successful in Austria. There, after fifteen years of unenthusiastically attempting to work a democratic system, the Austrian Catholic sub-culture went over almost *en bloc* to a form of fascism. The Christian Social party and the Catholic trade unions were dissolved and subsumed in a monolithic Fatherland Front. The Catholic hierarchy acquiesced in the change, and Catholics largely ran the new regime, which lasted until it was swallowed up by the Nazis in 1938. In Italy, too, the impact of fascism was devastating. There, the Italian Popular party was never strong enough to impose its vision on politics. By 1922, it had to choose between collaboration with the Socialists or with the Fascists. Hesitant and divided on the issue, it had to reckon with a new pope (Pius XI, 1922–39) who had no doubt where he stood. Though Pius XI had reservations about fascism, it was to him far and away a lesser evil than socialism. He approved the Fascist takeover of power and raised no objections even when the Popular party and the Catholic social organisations were abolished. Until Mussolini's fall in 1943, the Catholic Church could be considered – despite disputes on particular issues – one of the forces supporting the Fascist regime.

At the other extreme, there was a group of countries where Catholics could be considered on balance an anti-fascist force. In Switzerland, the decentralising and particularist traditions of the people, and not least the Catholic people, ensured that fascism had limited appeal. In the Netherlands, the Dutch Nazi party performed about as poorly in Catholic as in Protestant areas at its first electoral contest in 1935,[6] and the following year it was condemned by the Dutch Catholic hierarchy.[7] In Belgium, the Rexist movement, of fascist leanings, made serious inroads into the Catholic electorate at the general election of 1936; but at a by-election in 1937 Cardinal van Roey of Malines called on the people to vote against it, and thereafter it fell back.

The countries where the Catholic record is hardest to evaluate are Germany and France. In Germany, the Nazis had consistently poorer election results in Catholic areas than in Protestant, and in 1931 the bishops of the various German church provinces successively warned Catholics against the errors of Nazism.[8] Once the Nazis had reached power by legal means, the legitimacy of their authority was accepted; the prohibition on Catholics joining their party was rescinded; the dissolution of Catholic parties and social organisations was acquisced in; and in short the whole apparatus of closed Catholicism was abandoned. In France during the twenties, a society known as *Action française,* which combined a fascist-style ideology with an intransigent Catholicism, won support from many Catholics. In 1926, Pius XI condemned it on the ground that it was doctrinally incompatible with Catholicism, and it thenceforth lost ground. Yet in 1940, when Marshal Pétain achieved power by legal means and established an authoritarian regime, the Catholic hierarchy welcomed his accession and, at any rate at the outset, was one of the bulwarks of the government.

The inroads made by fascism on closed Catholicism reached their peak during the Second World War. By the end of 1940, Fascist regimes had been installed either by legal accession to power or by conquest in Italy, Germany, Austria, the Netherlands, Belgium and France. In all these countries, confessional political parties, trade unions, and many other confessional organisations had been suppressed. Only in Switzerland did the apparatus of a closed Catholicism survive. Elsewhere, Catholics had only two political courses open to them: they could join the official parties, labour fronts, and other organisations; or they could join the resistance.

Considerable numbers of them chose the second course. Catholics were prominent in the resistance movement of several countries. Men like Georges Bidault in France or Claus von Stauffenberg in Germany are well-known examples. This activity brought a further danger to closed Catholicism, for in the resistance movements Catholics rubbed shoulders with communists, liberals and social democrats. The breaking-down of barriers which had occurred during the First World War was repeated on a greater scale. A feeling spread among the resistance fighters that they must never again let their differences of outlook divide them. Enthusiasm spread for broad radical coalitions, in which Catholics, socialists, liberals and even communists could combine.

At the end of the war, the new spirit was widespread. Almost everywhere, Catholic political leaders sought to de-emphasise their links with the Church. In France, a new party was founded, led by militant Catholics and basing its policy on Catholic social thought; but it refused to describe itself as Catholic or even Christian in its title or its statutes, adopting instead the neutral label of *Mouvement républicain populaire* (MRP). In Austria, once the home of a particularly closed Catholicism, the Christian Social party was not restored. Its place was taken by a new grouping with a non-confessional title, the Austrian People's party, which proclaimed in its statutes that it had no link with any previously existing party. Shortly afterwards, the Austrian bishops announced that they and their clergy would take no further part in politics. In Belgium, some Catholics founded a new non-sectarian party, the *Union démocrate belge,* which they hoped would develop along the lines of the British Labour party. Cardinal van Roey opposed it, and it withered away, but he acquiesced in the Belgian Catholic party being reconstructed under the title Christian Social party as a formally nonconfessional body. In the Netherlands, too, the bishops insisted on Catholics retaining their separate organisation: the Catholic People's party was the only party in Europe to retain the word 'Catholic' in its title. Even there, much discussion went on among Catholics about the possibility of a breakthrough to non-sectarian groupings on the Anglo-Saxon model, and a few Catholics joined the Dutch Labour party. The most dramatic change occurred in Germany, where the great majority of the Catholic leaders – with the approval of their bishops – moved to establish an interconfessional party, the Christian Democratic Union, appealing to Protestants as well as Catholics. Only a few Catholics remained faithful to the Centre party, which withered away during the nineteen-fifties. In Italy alone was the trend in the opposite direction: there, the new Christian Democratic party had closer links with the Church than the old Popular party had maintained.

Some of the social organisations, too, were affected by the new desire for unity. This was particularly visible among trade unions. In Italy, Germany and Austria, Christians, social democrats and communists for a time united in a common organisation. In Belgium, the Netherlands and France, discussions for unity broke down, and the Christian trade unions retained their identities. Even in these countries, a greater degree of common action seemed apparent than before the war. In the Netherlands, for instance, a federal council was set up linking the socialist, Catholic and Protestant unions. Thus by the immediate post-war period, about 1945–6, Catholics in many parts of Europe seemed to be moving away from the closed end of the spectrum.

Yet, during the very years when multiple forces were eating away at closed Catholicism, other forces were working to build it up. One of the most important was the growing distinctiveness of Catholic social doctrine. In the last chapter it was explained how the encyclical *Rerum novarum* of 1891 had marked an important stage in the crystallisation of Catholic social teaching. Previously, Catholics had been divided between two schools of thought, laissez-faire and interventionist. The encyclical, by coming down in favour of the interventionist school, had helped to differentiate Catholics from other conservatives. This still left open the question of what form state intervention should take. During the ensuing forty years, Catholic social thinkers greatly developed their ideas on this subject and, once again, came to be grouped in two main camps.

As names for these two camps we can adopt the labels sometimes applied in the German-speaking countries – *Sozialpolitik* and *Sozialreform.*[9] The *Sozialpolitik* school was the more moderate. It accepted the basic framework of the capitalist system and wished only to adapt the system so as to make it more just. *Sozialpolitik* thinkers favoured a strong social insurance system, to safeguard against the vicissitudes of sickness, old age and unemployment. They also believed in the right of workers to organise themselves: most of the Christian trade-union leaders belonged to their ranks. By the nineteen-twenties and thirties, there was little distinctive about *Sozialpolitik* ideas. They were part of the stock-in-trade of most European democratic politicians and made coalition with social democrats and liberals quite practicable. Perhaps the most distinctive *Sozialpolitik* idea was the promotion of family allowances, which would equalise the burdens of large and small families. If family allowances were added to the social-security system of many European countries in the mid-twentieth century, this was largely due to Catholic influences.

The *Sozialreform* school was more intransigent. It believed that capitalist society was radically diseased and could not be cured just by modifications. The basic disease was the cult of individualism, which led to selfishness, acquisitiveness, the unjust distribution of wealth, and the brutal dislocations of the trade cycle. So far, *Sozialreform* thinkers might sound like socialists; but they were as far from socialism as they were from capitalism, for they felt that the socialist remedy was as bad as the disease. Socialists, too, preached conflict: the only difference was that they preached it between classes, not individuals. Their goal was revolution, which would prove as cruel and unjust as had capitalism. What the *Sozialreform* school stood for, compared to both capitalism and socialism, was harmony between individuals and between classes. It proposed to achieve this by strengthening what it deemed the natural and organic groups in society and giving them institutions where these did not exist. This meant, in particular, developing corporations, in which employers and employees of every branch of industry could jointly make the decisions on which their common welfare depended.

The contrast between *Sozialpolitik* and *Sozialreform* is, of course, oversimplified. They were not two hermetically distinct schools, but shaded into each other, with many Catholics being at some intermediate point in the spectrum. None the less, differences in tendency were visible. The *Sozialreform* school was strongest in Austria, with considerable support also in France and Italy. The *Sozialpolitik* school was more influential in Germany, the Netherlands, Belgium and Switzerland. There were also variations over time. In the relatively prosperous twenties, when capitalism seemed to be securing a recovery from wartime scarcity, *Sozialpolitik* prevailed; but in the depression-laden thirties, when the drawbacks of capitalism became more evident than ever before, the more drastic prescriptions of *Sozialreform* came into vogue.

Once again, it fell to a pope to adjudicate between rival Catholic schools. In 1931, Pius XI issued an encyclical on social questions, *Quadragesimo anno. Quadragesimo anno,* as its name implies, marked the fortieth anniversary of *Rerum novarum,* and was designed to bring the now ageing prescriptions of Leo XIII up to date. In it, Pius XI endorsed the idea of corporate organisation of society. He thus came down decisively in favour of the *Sozialreform* school of thought.

The implications of this decision took some time to work out. Initially, it appeared to obscure rather than clarify the boundaries between Catholic social thought and other ideologies. This was because fascism, for reasons of its own, had developed a similar attachment to corporatist principles. During the thirties and early forties the boundary between Fascist thought and Catholic thought was accordingly blurred. With the downfall of fascism everywhere in continental

Europe at the end of the war, corporatism became a distinctively Catholic doctrine. By that time, the word 'corporatism' had fallen out of favour because of its Fascist connotations, but the principle, under the less controversial titles of 'vocational organisation' or 'professional organisation', was enthusiastically endorsed by Catholic thinkers and leaders. The result was that in the immediate post-war period Catholic social teaching had a more distinctive content than before or since. Ideologically, it provided the underpinning for a revival of closed Catholicism.

Another factor working to support a revival of closed Catholicism was the growth during the inter-war years of Catholic Action. In the previous chapter, a distinction was made between two types of Catholic social organisation: the interest group, and the ginger group. Of these, only the interest group operated at the interface between the Catholic community and society at large. The ginger group operated at one remove, as a stimulating agent within a non-confessional interest group. Catholic Action operated at yet one further remove from the wider society. Its members were not intended to take political stands at all. Instead they were expected, by prayer, good works, and the force of personal example, to bring Christ into their milieu.

Yet despite its non-political nature, Catholic Action had political effects. This was because of its importance as a training ground. Its members developed skills, such as administration, public speaking, and the conciliation of differences, which could be valuable to a politician. Thanks to their grounding in Catholic social thought, they acquired the motivation to seek a renewal of society by political action. True, this was not a new phenomenon: some of the more long-standing Catholic Action movements, like the *Association de la jeunesse catholique française,* had long been known as breeding-grounds for Catholic politicians. Encouraged by Pius XI, Catholic Action burgeoned after the First World War and thus had a greater influence than at any previous period. In particular, this was the heyday of the new organisations of specialised Catholic Action. The first and most important of these was the Young Christian Workers, founded in Belgium by Father (later Cardinal) Cardijn in 1925, which soon spread over Europe and beyond. It was imitated by the Young Christian Farmers and Young Christian Students. These specialised groups bred a generation of deeply committed, attractive and energetic Catholic leaders. At least some of them passed over into politics.

There are two countries where, to judge from the secondary literature, the growth of Catholic Action was particularly important politically. In Italy, Catholic Action was important because it survived. At a time when both the Popular party and most Catholic social organisations had been dissolved by the Fascist regime, Catholic Action was the only organisation which kept Catholics together and working as Catholics. In 1943, when the Christian Democratic party was founded, Catholic Action provided a framework on which it could build its organisation. After the war, the electoral workers for the Christian Democrats were provided by the Civic Committees, which – though formally distinct from Catholic Action – were recruited from it. In France, where Catholic Action was exceptionally vigorous in the inter-war years, its political effects seem to have been even greater. The immediate post-war years saw, for the first and only time in French history, a party of Catholic inspiration – the MRP – becoming a major force. The MRP was largely formed by former militants of Catholic Action: of fifty-two members of its leading party bodies in 1959, nearly forty had previously been prominent in Catholic Action or similar organisations.[10] Indeed, one authority states that, if the MRP was more successful than any similar party previously launched, 'the main reason seems to be the development of Catholic Action and associated groups since the 1930s'.[11]

Yet another factor came into play after the Second World War to help a revival of closed Catholicism. This was the eclipse of political forces on the right. Fascism was discredited in all the countries of continental Europe. Only in Italy did a Fascist party even survive, and there it never won more than six per cent of the popular vote. Even non-Fascist parties of the right suffered an eclipse at the end of the war. In France, the Moderates and Radical-Socialists (who despite their name were a grouping of the right-centre) fell far below their pre-war strength in the immediate post-war elections and never fully recovered the ground lost. In Germany, no party to the right of the Christian Democrats equalled the importance of the German National People's party under the Weimar Republic. In Italy, the Liberals retained only a fraction of their importance in pre-Fascist days with about three per cent of the vote. Part of the support secured by Christian Democrats after the war undoubtedly came from right-wing electors who had no positive enthusiasm for Christian Democratic ideals, but who voted for them as a lesser evil than Socialists or Communists.

A further factor which strengthened the tendencies towards closed Catholicism was the beginning of the Cold War, in the late nineteen-forties. In the immediate post-war period, Catholics actually served with Communists in the governments of France, Italy and Austria and developed more cordial relations with them elsewhere. In Italy and France, small but significant groups of *Chrétiens progressistes* emerged who, while holding fast to Catholicism, argued that the communist analysis of society was substantially just and in politics co-operated with the Communist party. If this trend had continued, it could have eroded the closed Catholic position. With the rise of the Cold War, however, this danger was removed. In 1947, Communists left the ruling coalitions in France, Italy and Austria. The condemnation by the pope in 1949 of all collaboration with communism made the Christian progressists' position untenable, and their movement withered away, not to revive until after the period covered by this chapter.

In one or two countries, a revival of closed Catholicism was helped by the unexpected re-emergence of an issue which had appeared to be played out. This was the question of state aid to denominational schools. Rising costs and aspirations led to increasing burdens on all school systems in the post-war world; and in countries where Catholic schools received no subsidy, or an incomplete one, this led to demands for an increase in state aid. In France, two measures providing state aid for denominational schools were passed in 1951 and 1959. Though a parliamentary majority was found for both measures, they were opposed by the traditionally secularist parties – Communists, Socialists and most of the Radicals –

thus giving a new lease of life to the fading division between clerical and anti-clerical. The greatest effect was seen in Belgium. There, a Christian Social minister of education increased the grants to Catholic schools in 1952. A Liberal–Socialist coalition partially revoked these grants in 1955, causing intense bitterness in the Catholic section of the electorate. At the general election of 1958, Catholics rallied round the Christian Social party, whose share of the vote rose by five per cent as compared with the previous general election. A reviving Flemish nationalist movement, which might have been a threat to Catholic unity, was sharply checked. Chastened by defeat, Liberals and Socialists negotiated with the Christian Socials a compromise which has endured. While the struggle lasted, it had the effect of re-polarising Belgian politics and driving Catholics back towards the closed end of the spectrum.

Another factor must be mentioned among those helping the trend towards closed Catholicism: the giving of votes to women. Although women won the vote in most European countries at the end of the First World War, they were still denied it in France, Italy and (except for particular minorities such as war widows) Belgium. At the end of the Second World War, however, these three countries extended the franchise to women, leaving Switzerland as the only European democracy which still denied it to them. Public opinion polls showed that, in the nineteen-fifties, women were markedly more likely to support parties of Catholic or Christian inspiration than were men.[12] In all these countries, then, the female vote helped to buttress closed Catholicism. The effect was particularly important in Italy. There, in contrast to the rest of continental Europe, the bulk of the Socialists remained allied, even after the beginning of the Cold War, with the Communists. Opinion polls indicated that the Communist–Socialist alliance commanded a majority among male voters. To the women's vote is due the long domination of Italian politics by the Christian Democrats.

A final indication of the revival of closed Catholicism in postwar Europe may be seen in the renewed willingness of some national hierarchies to give strong guidance to their flocks. This habit was not universal. In France, the trend was the other way: the last time that the French hierarchy had taken a strong line politically was in 1924–5, when it had rallied its flock against the anti-clerical measures of the Herriot government.[13] During the nineteen-fifties, French bishops usually confined themselves to urging support for candidates, regardless of party, who favoured Church schools.[14] During the general election of 1956, they forbade candidates to describe themselves as Catholics or to draw attention to their connections with Catholic organisations.[15] In Austria, as already mentioned, the hierarchy laid down a line of political neutrality, and although there are reports of some deviations from this,[16] on the whole it is clear that the bishops were much less active than before the war. The Swiss hierarchy, too, maintained its tradition of reserve.

Even in countries where the bishops did intervene at elections, there were normally limits beyond which they did not go. It was not common for bishops to express preferences between named political parties. The Dutch bishops were unusual in urging support for the Catholic People's party by name before the general elections of 1946 and 1948.[17] A careful student of German electoral pastorals has found only one instance where a bishop favoured the Christian Democrats by name: during the Rhineland–Palatinate communal elections of 1952, Bishop Stohr of Trier stated that bitter experience with regard to the protection of Catholic schools showed that only the Christian Democrats were trustworthy.[18] The normal practice in Germany has been simply to urge a vote for those who will support Christian principles.[19]

There were also limits to the application of sacramental discipline. It was certainly used *against* parties whose doctrines were regarded as incompatible with Christianity: the papal decree of 1949, refusing the sacraments to those who supported the Communist party or its allies, was intended to apply world-wide. It was less usual to employ such methods *in favour of* a particular party. The only examples I have come across occurred in Belgium, where before the general election of 1958 at least two bishops declared that to vote for any other party than the Christian Socials would be gravely sinful.[20] The Dutch bishops in 1954 refused the sacraments to anyone who joined the socialist trade unions, but they specifically stopped short of using the same sanction against anyone who supported the Socialist party.[21] Hubert Metz, in his study of German bishops' pronouncements, notes that in talking of misuse of the vote they preferred the words 'guilt' or 'responsibility' to the theologically more precise word 'sin'.[22] The analyses of Italian episcopal pronouncements published by Alfonso Prandi and Domenico Settembrini have not revealed any instances of bishops calling on the electors to vote for the Christian Democratic party by name.

Yet, it is possible to avoid naming a party while none the less conveying a clear recommendation to the voter. The following instruction to Italian voters from the Consistorial Congregation, published in 1945, provides an illustration:

> Catholics may give their vote only to those candidates or those lists of candidates of whom one has the certainty that they will respect and defend the observance of the divine law and the rights of religion and the Church in private and in public life.[23]

The reader would have little doubt that, in the eyes of the Congregation, only the Christian Democrats measured up to this standard.

On the whole, it seems probable that over much of continental Europe, the bishops imposed a more continuous direction on the voters in the period 1945–60 than they had generally done before. In Belgium, whose hierarchy had the strongest record in Europe for political intervention, the bishops seem to have gone to greater lengths during the school struggle of 1954–8 than they had at any time since the previous school struggle of 1879–84. In the Netherlands, the tradition of episcopal direction, already strong before the war, seems to have reached a climax after it. In Germany, the bishops developed the habit of publishing a *Wahlhirtenbrief* (a pastoral letter in connection with the elections), not only before every federal election, but before every *Land* and communal election as well. Perhaps the most active intervention occurred in Italy. Here a constant stream of advice came from individual bishops, from regional bishops' conferences, from the national hierarchy, from Vatican congregations, and from the pope. Not only at national elections, but at regional and communal ones, the faithful were repeatedly urged to maintain electoral unity behind a party committed to Christian principles – which could hardly mean otherwise than to vote Christian Democrat. There were also interventions on issues of policy. In 1952, Pius XII tried hard to persuade the Christian Democrat leader, Alcide de Gasperi, to form a common front with the Fascists in the Rome municipal elections, so as to obviate the risk of a Communist takeover in the Eternal City. Such an alliance would have gone against everything that de Gasperi stood for, but he had to withstand the most intense pressure before his view prevailed. In the late fifties, when some Christian Democrats, disenchanted by electoral setbacks and encouraged by a rift between Socialists and Communists, urged a broadening of the government by bringing in the Socialists, many churchmen strenously opposed the change, and succeeded in blocking it until past the period covered by this chapter. On the whole, it seems true that, at least in Germany, Italy and the Low Countries, electoral intervention by the Catholic hierarchies was more continuous and intensive in the period 1945–60 than in any previous period of equivalent length.

For all these reasons, closed Catholicism reached its peak of development in continental Europe after the Second World War. As far as political parties were concerned, the most striking gains were made in Italy and France. In Italy, where the Popular party of the pre-Fascist period had won only twenty per cent of the vote, the Christian Democrats averaged over forty per cent, reaching their highest result in 1948 with forty-eight per cent. In France, where there had never been a successful party of Catholic inspiration, the MRP averaged twenty-eight per cent of the vote in the three general elections of 1945–6 and was still running at a significant twelve per cent in 1958. In the smaller countries, gains were less dramatic because the Catholic parties had been better entrenched, but even there, they maintained or improved upon their previous record. In Belgium, the Christian Social party systematically gained more of the vote in the forties and fifties than the Catholic party had done in the twenties and thirties, the high water mark (forty-eight per cent) coming in 1950. In the Netherlands, the Catholic People's party marginally improved on the record of the pre-war Roman Catholic State party. Its highest point came as late as 1963, with 31.9 per cent of the votes. In Austria, the People's party in the forties and fifties averaged about three per cent higher than the Christian Social party had done in the twenties and thirties, achieving its best figure at the general election of 1945, with just under fifty per cent of the vote. In Switzerland, the Conservative People's party maintained and even fractionally increased its share of parliamentary representation, averaging twenty-three per cent of the vote in the elections of 1945–60.

The one country where the figures show a move away from a strong Catholic party was, of course, Germany. There, the decision to switch support from the Catholic Centre party to the interconfessional Christian Democrats meant that Catholics' influence within their chosen vehicle was attenuated. While Catholics provided about two-thirds of the Christian Democrats' electoral support, the Protestant minority was substantial and had influence even beyond its numerical strength. The party realised that, while it could rely on Catholic support, if it wished for a majority it must woo Protestants. During the fifties, there was some anxiety in Catholic circles at the attenuation of Catholic influence in the Christian Democratic party.[24] None the less, the attenuation brought its compensations. The Christian Democrats were much stronger than the Centre party had been, reaching fifty per cent of the vote in the general election of 1957. Instead of a controlling voice in a medium-sized party, German Catholics had gained an important voice in a large party. On balance, the forces of closed Catholicism had lost less ground than appeared at first sight.

The natural constituency of the parties of Catholic inspiration was the practising Catholic population. Before the nineteen-fifties, figures for the proportion of Catholics who practised their religion are hardly ever obtainable. During that decade data became more plentiful, and by the end of the fifties it is possible to make estimates for the proportion of practising Catholics in the various countries of continental Europe. If these are compared with the percentage of votes obtained by Christian Democrats at elections of the same period (see Table 2), a remarkable fact emerges. This is that parties of Catholic inspiration had, everywhere except in France, roughly reached the limits of their natural constituency. In some countries, notably Austria, it had even exceeded those limits. If party strength is the criterion, closed Catholicism had reached its maximum possible development.

Table 2. Percentage of practising Catholics and percentage of the Christian Democratic vote in the countries of continental Europe

Country	Approx. percentage of practising Catholics, 1960[a]	Percentage of votes won by Christian Democratic or Catholic party, at general election nearest to 1960
Austria	36	44 (1959)
Belgium	48	41[b] (1961)
France	23	12 (1958)
West Germany	23	45[c] (1961)
Italy	43	42 (1958)
The Netherlands	32	32 (1959)
Switzerland	21	23 (1959)

Notes

a. The sources from which this table is derived will be found in Appendix B. The approximate nature of the figures must be stressed. For most of the countries on the list, they may be several percentage points out.

b. The general election of 1961 was a disappointing one for the Christian-Social party. In 1958 it had gained 46.5 per cent of the vote. This gives a more accurate picture of its strength when a religious issue was prominent.

c. The Christian Democrats in West Germany appealed to Protestants as well as Catholics. None the less, this figure is impressive. It indicates that they appealed not only to practising Catholics, but to a number of nominal ones as well.

Catholic social organisations showed the same progress in post-war Europe as did Catholic parties. The youth movements of those parties showed impressive growth, especially in Germany and Italy. A family movement was strong in France and developing in other countries. Employers' groups and groups catering for professions such as doctors, teachers and lawyers developed in most countries.

Among farmers, the Catholic interest groups already existing in the Netherlands and Belgium were joined by one in Switzerland, founded in 1942.[25] Elsewhere Catholic or Catholic-inspired ginger groups existed within non-denominational interest groups.[26]

The progress of closed Catholicism was particularly visible in the workers' movements. The post-war attempt to build united labour movements in Italy, Germany and Austria survived only in the last-named country; in Italy unity was broken in 1948 and in Germany in 1955. In Germany, the revived Christian unions had limited success: with only two per cent of the total trade-union membership, they fell far short of the twenty per cent achieved by Christian trade unions in the days before Hitler.[27] However, Catholic influence in the general trade union movement was kept alive by an active ginger group, the *katholische Arbeiterbewegung*. In Italy, success was greater. There Catholics helped to form the CISL, a formally non-confessional interest group with a social-democrat element, but in practice largely Catholic, which mobilised about thirty-five per cent of the organised labour force. Alongside it, they maintained a fully Catholic ginger group, the ACLI. Even in Austria, where the united trade-union organisation survived, it had a federal structure in which the Christian unions maintained their identity. In France and the Netherlands, Catholic unions increased their proportionate strength. In Switzerland, they were at about the same point. In Belgium, they forged ahead until by the end of the decade they were the largest trade-union body, well ahead of their principal rivals, the socialist unions.

Finally, the importance of closed Catholicism in continental Europe can be seen from the prominence of its leaders and the impact of its policies. All prime ministers of Italy in the fifteen years after 1945 were Christian Democrats, as were all chancellors of Austria. In Germany, the first chancellor of the new German Federal Republic was the Catholic leader of the Christian Democratic party, Konrad Adenauer. In the Netherlands, the Catholic party provided the prime minister (L. J. M. Beel) from 1946 to 1948 and was represented in all post-war governments. In Belgium, the Christian Social party governed, or shared in the government of, the country from 1947 to 1954 and again after 1958. In Switzerland, the Catholic Conservative party regularly provided two out of the seven members of the federal executive. In France, the MRP provided the prime minister for only brief periods, but it was represented in most governments of the Fourth Republic; and two of its members, Georges Bidault and Robert Schuman, almost monopolised the important portfolio of foreign affairs for the ten years 1944–54. Like other leaders, these men had their critics. People complained of Adenauer's overbearing manner, of Bidault's indecisiveness, of the ineffectiveness of most Italian prime ministers after de Gasperi (1945–54) – and indeed of de Gasperi himself in his last years. But for good or ill, organised Catholicism played a more influential role politically on the continent of Europe between 1945 and about 1960 than ever before or since.

The influence on policy was unmistakable. One major aim of Christian Democratic parties during these years was to implement Catholic social teaching by establishing or strengthening vocational organisation in their respective countries. In this endeavour they had substantial success. In Germany, Austria, France, Italy, Belgium and the Netherlands, legislation either established or strengthened joint consultation at the level of the individual plant. At the level of industry as a whole, success was somewhat less widespread, but even there organs of joint consultation were developed in the Netherlands, Belgium and France. Another favoured cause of the Christian Democrats was European unity, which made great strides in this period, culminating with the establishment of the European Economic Community in 1958. True, Christian Democrats were not the only people working for codetermination in industry or for a united Europe; but neither cause would have gone so far without the support of the Christian Democrats, who were the largest single bloc in the parliaments of continental Europe.

The Anglo-American world, too, was affected by some of the forces which strengthened a closed Catholicism in continental Europe. Catholic social teaching underwent the same development, and *Quadragesimo anno* was studied by Anglo-

American Catholics as well as European ones. Catholic Action underwent a similar expansion. Rising costs and expectations produced similar demands for state aid to Catholic schools; and in the United States, Britain, Australia and some provinces of Canada, Catholic education became in the fifties a more active political issue than it had been for several decades.

Furthermore, some of the factors *retarding* the growth of closed Catholicism in Europe had less effect in Anglo-America. Fascism had a less disintegrating effect on Catholic unity because it was of less importance. The nearest thing to a Catholic fascist demagogue to appear in any Anglo-American country was the American Father Charles Coughlin, who enjoyed a wide radio audience; but when his influence was tested at the presidential elections of 1936, the candidate he favoured won less than two per cent of the vote. The mood of unity engendered by shared adversity during the two world wars reached less deep in the Anglo-American countries, which were spared invasion and occupation, than in some parts of Europe.

Not surprisingly, then, some movement towards a closed Catholicism occurred even in the Anglo-American world during the period covered by this chapter. Of the few examples of *de facto* Catholic parties in these countries listed in Chapter 1, most originated during this period – the Democratic party in New South Wales, the Centre party in Liverpool, the Nationalists in Northern Ireland, the *Union nationale* in Quebec, the Democratic Labor party in Australia. Catholic social organisations developed too. Catholic employers' associations appeared in England (1938) and Canada (1943). A National Catholic Rural Life Conference was active in the United States and a similar body in Australia. In the maritime provinces of Canada, the Antigonish movement, which while formally non-confessional was in practice heavily Catholic, developed agricultural co-operatives. Ireland saw an influential rural renewal movement, *Muintir na tíre* ('people of the land'), which was formally non-confessional, but which was founded by a Catholic priest and drew on Catholic social teaching for its ideas. In the labour field, Catholic unions became a major force in French

Canada. In Ireland, where the trade-union movement had developed as non-sectarian, it split in 1945. The breakaway group, the Congress of Irish Unions, differentiated itself from the larger Irish Trade Union Congress by appearing more Catholic as well as more nationalist – though it is fair to say that many Catholic workers remained loyal to the Irish Trade Union Congress.

A feature of Anglo-American Catholicism was the growth of an intellectual movement. Canada adopted the French device of the *semaine sociale* in 1920. The United States built up a network of labour schools on a diocesan and sometimes parochial basis in the nineteen-thirties. In England, the Catholic Workers' College at Oxford was established in 1921. Ireland had its own Catholic Workers' College from 1948. In Australia, the bishops set aside one Sunday of each year as Social Justice Sunday, and on it issued a statement about some social problem – education, immigration, communism, and so on.

A further sign of the growth of closed Catholicism in the Anglo-American world was a revived readiness on the part of hierarchies to give guidance to their flocks in political matters. At the organisational level, it is true, clergy were less important in this period than the last. Even in Ireland and Quebec, where they had been most active, they now left electioneering almost entirely to the laity. At the level of guidance on principle, however, the Church was still prepared to intervene. This was most likely to happen on the education issue: American, British and Australian bishops made repeated complaints about the financial difficulties of Catholic schools. In some countries, other issues came up. In Canada, some of the bishops in 1934 condemned the new socialist party in that country, the Co-operative Commonwealth Federation, for embracing doctrines contrary to Catholic social teaching. However the CCF toned down its language, and in 1943 the hierarchy rescinded the ban.[28] In Ireland, the hierarchy in 1951 condemned a proposed maternity-and-child-welfare scheme as contrary to Catholic social teaching. The government withdrew the scheme, and the minister responsible resigned. In the United States, bishops and clergy in the nineteen-forties helped to block a proposed repeal of the Massachusetts law forbidding the dissemination of birth-control information.[29] In Australia, there was a particularly rich crop of episcopal statements at the time of the Labor party split in the fifties. Its effect was blurred, however, by the fact that not all the bishops said the same thing. Some, like Archbishop Mannix of Melbourne, warned against supporting the Australian Labor party; others, like Cardinal Gilroy of Sydney, stated that Catholics were free to vote for any party except the Communist.

On the whole, however, Catholics in the Anglo-American world remained towards the open end of the spectrum during the period covered by this chapter. Clerical intervention in politics, while not unknown, remained well below the level of continental Europe. Catholic social organisations were mostly of the ginger-group rather than the interest-group type, and fell well short of the most effective organisations on the continent. The Association of Catholic Trade Unionists in the United States, for instance – a country with many millions of Catholic workers – seems never to have had more than fifteen chapters.[30] The *de facto* Catholic political parties of the period all had a narrow geographical base or attracted only a minority of Catholic voters, or both. On the whole, Catholics remained loyal to the pattern built up in the previous generation: they backed the more left-wing of the two major parties in a two-party system. As one student of voting behaviour has put it: 'In the United States, they were disproportionately Democratic; in Great Britain and Australia, Labour; in Canada, Liberal'.[31] In New Zealand, the absence of nationwide surveys made assessment more difficult, but evidence from constituency surveys suggests that a tendency for Catholics to vote Labour, while less marked than in Australia, was in evidence.[32] In Ireland, an overwhelmingly Catholic country, all parties were more or less equally Catholic.

In this chapter as in the last, it is important not to exaggerate the differences between continental Europe and Anglo-America. In both groups of countries, the direction of movement was the same – from open Catholicism towards closed. But the movement was much more vigorous in the former than the latter. It was in the period covered by this chapter that the gap between Catholics in continental Europe and those in the Anglo-American countries reached its widest point.

5

Variations over time: The decay of closed Catholicism, c. 1960–

In continental Europe, the nineteen-sixties and early seventies saw a notable shift away from closed Catholicism. Christian Democratic parties everywhere became less powerful, or less confessional, or both. In France, Christian Democracy disappeared altogether as a separate force: the once powerful MRP formally ceased to act as a political party in 1967, and Christian Democrats are now no more than a tendency within President Giscard d'Estaing's *Union pour la démocratie française*.[1] In the Netherlands, the Catholic People's party lost nearly half its votes in less than ten years, falling from thirty-two per cent of the vote in 1963 to eighteen per cent in 1972. In Belgium, the decline of the Christian Social party was almost as spectacular: from 46.5 per cent of the vote in 1963 to thirty per cent in 1971. In Switzerland, the Conservative-Christian-Social party (as the Conservative party re-named itself in 1957) lost ground only slightly: from its peak of forty-eight seats out of 200 in 1963, it dropped back to forty-four out of 200 in 1971. However, an analysis by age cohort based on data collected in 1972 suggested that support for the party was strikingly less among young practising Catholics than among old or middle-aged ones.[2]

Elsewhere, Christian Democratic parties maintained their strength more successfully, but only by dint of diminishing their confessional character. The German Christian Democrats remained a powerful party, in 1965 almost equalling their share of seats of twelve years earlier, before falling back slightly in the general elections of 1969 and 1972. But they were evolving more and more into a catch-all party of the right, like the British Conservatives. As a result, they became increasingly unattractive to left-wing Catholic and increasingly appealing to right-wing Protestants. The situation of the nineteen-fifties reversed itself. Whereas formerly the Christian Democrats could count on the Catholic vote and had to woo Protestants, now they could count on conservative Protestants but had to work to retain Catholic support.[3] In Austria, the People's party remained strong, reaching its apogee as late as 1966, though declining gradually thereafter. Like its German counterpart, it tended to become a general conservative party, appealing to many besides committed Catholics. A poll in 1965–6 indicated that thirty-five per cent of People's party voters were not practising Catholics.[4] The case of Italy is particularly intriguing. There, the Christian Democrats, despite complaints of corruption and economic mismanagement, have confounded many observers by maintaining their strength. At four successive elections between 1963 and 1976 they retained approximately thirty-nine per cent of the vote. This stability, however, masked a considerable shift in social base. Two polls taken with a seven-year interval between them showed that whereas in 1968 eighty-five per cent of Christian Democrat voters claimed to attend Church often, in 1975 only sixty-five per cent claimed to do so.[5] R. E. M. Irving has noted that in the late seventies the Christian Democratic party was much less dependent on the Church than it had been thirty years before,[6] and Samuel Barnes stated bluntly: 'the Catholic subculture and the Christian Democratic electorate should not be equated. The latter is larger than the former.'[7] In other words, considerable numbers of lapsed or indifferent Catholics support the Christian Democrats, not because it is a religious party, but because it is a relatively right-wing party.

Catholic social organisations, too, declined in importance or became less confessional during the sixties. In Germany, the Christian trade unions, already feeble, suffered a blow when in 1966 two of their largest affiliates decided to join the neutral trade unions.[8] In Italy there was serious discussion at the beginning of the seventies of re-uniting the Communist-dominated CGIL with the Catholic-dominated CISL in one organisation. In France, the Christian trade-union movement, the CFTC, reconstituted itself in 1964 as a secular movement, the CFDT or French Democratic Confederation of

Labour. In the Netherlands, many of the Catholic social organisations amalgamated with sister organisations from other traditions. For instance, the Catholic employers' association fused with the Protestant one, while the Catholic labour unions federated with the socialist ones. In Belgium, the Catholic social organisations held up well in numbers, but three Louvain sociologists estimated that thirty per cent of their membership was unintegrated or weakly integrated in the Catholic Church.[9]

Another aspect of the swing towards open Catholicism in continental Europe during the sixties was that the Catholic hierarchies became more discreet in guiding their flocks on how to vote. The last time that the French hierarchy seems to have given any guidance was at the time of the referendum on the new constitution in 1958, when it told the electors that, despite the description in the text of France as a 'lay republic', they were still entitled to vote for it.[10] In Belgium, the general election of 1961 was reported as being the first since 1884 at which the hierarchy gave no guidance to the electors on how they ought to vote.[11] In the Netherlands, the hierarchy also relapsed into silence, and in 1967 the Bishop of 's-Hertogenbosch went so far as to say that religious parties were outdated.[12] The German hierarchy was slower to move than some, but in 1969 it announced that henceforward it would not feel obliged to issue a pastoral letter on the occasion of every election.[13] The Italian hierarchy showed least movement, but even it offered vaguer guidance in the general elections of 1963 and 1968 than it had done before.

Where hierarchies did maintain the old style of intervention, they had some spectacular disappointments. Three main instances occurred in the late sixties and early seventies. The first was in Belgium. Of all the countries covered in this book, this was the one where the hierarchy was most accustomed to having its voice heeded. It had repeatedly and successfully imposed unity on the Catholic vote. The Daensists felt its weight before 1914, the Rexists in 1937, the UDB in 1945, the Flemish Nationalists in 1932 and 1958. In 1966, the hierarchy moved with accustomed confidence to resolve an issue that had arisen with its baliwick. In reply to demands that the Catholic University of Louvain be separated into distinct French- and Dutch-language universities, it insisted on the continued unity of the university. This produced such an explosion of anger among Flemish Catholics that the hierarchy had to reverse its decision. Moreover, the episode appears to have made a lasting change in its political behaviour. As one Flemish Jesuit put it, 'the reaction of Flemish Catholic opinion was so vehement, unanimous and determined that it has probably put a final end to a particular kind of pastoral letter.'[14]

A few years later it was the turn of the Italian bishops to suffer a rebuff. In 1970 against Christian Democratic opposition, the Italian parliament passed an act allowing for the first time in Italy a limited measure of divorce. The Italian constitution allows the opponents of a particular measure, if they can obtain enough signatures, to demand a referendum on it. Parish priests and Catholic Action organisations quickly set about collecting the necessary signatures and before long had more than enough to secure their referendum. It took place in 1974, preceded by an appeal from the Italian bishops to the electors to vote for a repeal of the divorce law. To the general surprise, the law was upheld by a three-to-two majority. It was the sharpest demonstration that the Italian bishops had had since 1945 of the limits to their political power.

The third country in which the hierarchy suffered a disappointment was Germany. In the early seventies, the socialist-liberal coalition then in office introduced a bill to legalise abortion. This induced the Catholic hierarchy to abandon the neutrality adopted in the 1969 elections. Before the general election of 1972, it issued an appeal to the electorate in effect asking it to vote Christian Democratic so as to secure the defeat of the bill. The appeal was a failure. The governing coalition increased its share of the vote in Catholic as well as Protestant areas. The widespread popularity of the government's policy of conciliation with East Germany seems to have more than made up for any opposition it might have aroused by its support for abortion.

The withdrawal by bishops from electoral intervention was not necessarily accompanied by a disengagement from politics altogether. Before the nineteen-sixties, most episcopal statements had been concerned with two subject areas: the defence of the rights of the Church (above all its right to teach) and the defence of traditional Catholic morality (above all in the area of sex and marriage). During the sixties, there was a movement away from these areas towards a concern with the wider needs of society. It was becoming increasingly accepted that issues such as pollution, cultural autonomy, poverty in the Third World were moral issues on which the Church had a right and a duty to speak.[15] But these pronouncements, often in general terms, were a far cry from a call to support a particular political party; they no longer underpinned a closed Catholicism.

Many reasons can be found for this decline of closed Catholicism. Perhaps the earliest to operate was an evolution in European social democracy. The social democratic tradition on the continent was anti-clerical, even atheistic: a result partly of past conflicts and partly of the Marxist philosophy from which social democrats, to varying extents, derived their principles. Whereas between the wars Social Democrats and Christian Democrats had (except in Weimar Germany and intermittently in Belgium) been in opposition to each other, in post-war Europe they were generally allies. In the Netherlands, France, Belgium and the German *Laender,* Christian Democrats and Social Democrats were frequently in government together. In Austria, the coalition took on an almost permanent nature: People's party and Socialist party formed a two-party government from 1947 to 1966. In Switzerland, Catholics and Socialists served together in the government (along with Radicals and Farmers) from 1943 to 1953 and again after 1959. In Italy, the bulk of the socialists, led by Pietro Nenni, remained in opposition through the fifties; but a substantial minority, under Giuseppe Saragat, remained in alliance with the Christian Democrats, and by the early sixties even the Nenni socialists were moving towards a Christian Democrat alliance. Many socialists, too, were moving away philosophically from their Marxist roots. Finally, a pragmatic consideration affected socialist perceptions. Social Democrats hoped to come to power by democratic means. Since the working class formed a majority of the electorate in all European democracies, they might hope to attain this objective by capitalising on the workers' class consciousness. In Italy and France, it is true, the main obstacle to achieving this aim was the competition of an even stronger Communist party. In other European countries where communism was weak, the main obstacle was the distrust which socialist anti-clericalism aroused in the substantial segment of the working class which remained loyal to the churches.

For all these reasons, the post-war period saw among Social Democrats what might be described as a process of 'de-anti-clericalisation'.[16] The change was least visible in France and Italy, where socialists feared that any reduction in their militancy would result in losses to the Communists. It came perhaps most emphatically in Austria, where the Vienna programme of 1958 marked a decisive break with the socialists' anti-clerical past, and in Germany, where the Godesberg programme of 1959 showed a similar, if less marked, toning down of old slogans. It had come even earlier in the Netherlands, where immediately after the war the socialists had changed their name to the Labour party and had hoped to recruit progressive Catholics and Protestants to their ranks. In Belgium, there was no formal change of policy on this scale, but by agreeing to the school pact of 1958, Social Democrats took a step in the same direction. These developments took time to bear fruit, for there was widespread suspicion among Catholics about the sincerity of the socialists' new line. In the long run they made it easier for Catholics to vote socialist and harder for Catholic bishops to tell them not to do so.

The process of 'de-anti-clericalisation' also affected some of the continental Liberal parties. Like the socialists, they wished to expand their electoral base, and, like the socialists, some of them saw the best hope of doing this in purging themselves of traditional anti-clericalism and appealing to the Catholic vote. The process was most evident in Belgium, where in 1961 the Liberal party changed its name, rewrote its statutes, and was rewarded by picking up Catholic votes. In Italy, the small Liberal party – in contrast to the more numerous Liberals of pre-Fascist days – preferred to distinguish itself from the Christian Democrats by a free-market economic policy, rather than by stressing issues of Church and state. In France, the Radicals divided in two: while one section remained resolutely lay and preferred to ally with Socialists and even Communists, the other section, under Jean-Jacques Servan-Schreiber, was prepared first to collaborate and then in 1971 to merge with the remnants of Christian Democracy.

Meanwhile, even Communists were edging closer towards Catholicism. As the Cold War gave way to détente in the sixties, bitter feelings on both sides were softening. The change was most important in Italy, where the Communists had the strongest mass following in western Europe, and had a real hope of achieving office by democratic means if they could allay Catholic suspicions. Moreover, unlike Communists elsewhere, they had a tradition of respect for Church interests. Even in the post-war debates on the Italian consitution, they had voted for continuing the concordat which the Vatican had negotiated with Mussolini in 1929. During the sixties, their efforts began to pay off. In 1963, Pope John XXIII received in audience Alexis Adzhubei, son-in-law of the Soviet leader Khrushchev. After that it was harder for Italian bishops to denounce communism in such unmeasured terms as before. In the four general elections of 1963, 1968, 1972 and 1976, the Communist vote showed a steady advance. This may have been in part because of their persistent reassurance of the Catholic electorate.

While some Communists appeared to be edging towards the right, some Catholics were moving far towards the left. This trend was most evident among the younger clergy and lay intellectuals. While not so strong as in Latin America, it was by the late sixties noticeable in most parts of continental Europe. A movement called Christians for Socialism gained members in several countries. In France, the Socialist party, once so anti-clerical, was being colonised by Catholics who were often among the more left-wing of its activists.[17] In the Netherlands, a group of Catholics formed the nucleus of a new left-wing grouping, the Radical party, launched in 1968. In Italy, individual Catholics were by 1976 standing as independents on Communist electoral lists.[18] The numerical strength of this movement must not be exaggerated. Opinion polls indicate that the proportion of practising Catholics who were prepared to vote for Socialist or Communist parties was still a small minority. An authoritative French observer calculated that, of the forty thousand French priests in 1972, perhaps one thousand had shown political engagement.[19] Though few in number, they were vocal and made it harder for bishops or lay politicians to rally Catholics round a common political position, even if they wished to do so.

In practice, clerical and political leaders probably did not even wish to do so, for another feature of this period was a decline in the distinctiveness of Catholic social teaching. So long as Catholics believed that they possessed a body of doctrine which marked them out from socialists on the one hand and capitalists on the other, they had good reason for congregating in parties and social organisations with a distinctively Catholic basis. If their social teaching ceased to be distinguishable from that of other groups, then a major motive for separate organisation would disappear. This appears to have been happening in the fifties and sixties.

To some extent, it was the result of success: Catholics ceased to have distinctive objectives because their objectives were fulfilled. As was shown in the last chapter, the principal prescription of Catholic social teaching – the establishment of vocational or corporate organisation – was in considerable measure achieved in continental Europe after the war. More important, however, was the increasing irrelevance of this teaching to the problems of the day. Corporatist doctrine had been developed as a remedy for class conflict. It was appropriate to a period when class conflict appeared one of the most serious problems facing industrial societies. In the fifties and most of the sixties, this was no longer true: the working classes were becoming more affluent, strikes were less frequent, the spectre of unemployment was replaced by a scarcity of labour. Other problems came to the fore: reconstruction of war-damaged economies, the care of migrant labour, the maintenance of economic growth. By the end of the sixties, attention was turning to the control of inflation and care of the environment. On none of these issues had Catholic social thought anything distinctive to say. The point can be illustrated by referring to the major papal pronouncements of the period. *Mater et magistra* of 1961 was the first encyclical on social questions since *Quadragesimo anno* of 1931. It hardly mentioned corporate organisation, except to remark that it had pitfalls of its own. Indeed it made few specific recommendations: on the whole, it ratified the then prevailing consensus in advanced societies – the desirability of governmental management of the economy, the need for reducing regional disparities, the importance of economic aid to the underdeveloped world, and so on. The two remaining social encyclicals of the sixties, *Pacem in terris* (1963) and *Populorum progressio* (1967), were notable as marking a developoment of the Church's interest in fresh fields – international relations and the Third World respectively. They did not have any very distinctive recommendations to offer. In a letter to commemorate the eightieth anniversary of *Rerum Novarum,* entitled *Octogesima adveniens* (1971), Paul VI specifically abandoned the attempt to provide a comprehensive social doctrine: 'In view of the varied situations in the world, it is difficult to give one teaching to cover them all or to offer a solution which has universal value. This is not our intention or even our mission.'[20]

The change in the intellectual climate of Catholicism was accelerated by the Second Vatican Council (1962–5). The Council was not primarily concerned with politics, but the ferment of change and controversy which it unleashed in the Catholic world was bound to spill over into the political field. The dialogue with Protestants and non-believers which it encouraged was not easy to reconcile with the maintenance of a closed Catholicism in the political arena. The teaching of the Council's decree on the Church and the modern world, *Gaudium et spes,* with its openness to insights from other intellectual traditions and its generally optimistic tone, seemed to undermine the assumptions on which closed Catholicism had been built. The unprecedented degree of controversy between Catholics which the Council stimulated made Catholics more likely to question old assumptions in politics as in other matters.

This was well illustrated in the field of education. The policy of the Catholic Church had long been to insist that wherever possible Catholic children be educated in Catholic schools, and that such schools were entitled to financial support from the state. On the whole, it had been successful in mobilising the Catholic electorate behind this stand. An alternative point of view was however, possible even within the fold of traditional Catholicism. It could be argued that to gather Catholic children in Catholic schools meant to neglect the Church's duty to those Catholic children who for one reason or another could not attend such schools, and indeed to the wider community beyond them. It could also be argued that concentration on school-building meant neglecting other forms of apostolate. In France, there was a tradition among Catholics reaching at least to the nineteen-thirties which raised such issues.[21] After the Council, these questionings became a flood. In the Netherlands, where one of the most comprehensive Catholic school systems had been built up, an opinion poll published in 1971 reported that forty-four per cent of Catholic parents would prefer interdenominational schools to Catholic ones.[22] In Belgium, a considerable section of the Christian Social party was by the late sixties questioning the commitment to Catholic schools. In several German *Laender*, legislation was passed with the support of Christian Democratic deputies and despite protests from the bishops, providing for the merger of Protestant and Catholic school systems. This kind of questioning could, if unchecked, have almost as corrosive an effect on the maintenance of Catholic unity as the decline of a distinctive Catholic social doctrine. In most continental countries, a major reason for the development of Catholic political parties had been to defend the Catholic school. If that was no longer considered a desirable objective, there was less reason than ever for maintaining distinctive Catholic parties.

Another reason for the decline of closed Catholicism may be that, with experience, its drawbacks became increasingly evident to the Church authorities. For such drawbacks undoubtedly existed. Leaders of Christian Democratic parties or Catholic interest groups could develop an independent power base which made them slow to heed the desires of pope or bishops. We have already seen how de Gasperi rejected the policy pressed on him by Pius XII at the time of the Rome municipal elections of 1952. Konrad Adenauer, Chancellor of

Germany from 1949 to 1963, was also difficult to handle. 'Excellent Catholic . . . but critical of Church authorities – "too demanding"', wrote the papal nuncio about him.[23] Worse still, if Catholic parties or social organisations became involved in corruption, then the Church was likely to be dragged in too. In 1958, Cardinal Ottaviani, one of the architects of ecclesiastical support for Christian Democracy, frankly pointed to the consequences:

> Everyone goes to the bishops, making them pressurisers of those in power, and thus a wariness develops in the country towards the men of eternity transformed into agents of temporal things. This is not the way to honour the Church. Rather it dishonours her. This is not to serve the Church, but to serve oneself.[24]

A final reason may be suggested for the shift from a closed towards an open Catholicism in recent years. This is the declining demographic base for a closed Catholicism. Wherever figures are available, they show an erosion of Catholic religious practice. In Austria, the decline has been relatively slight – from thirty-seven per cent in 1960 to thirty-three per cent in 1975.[25] In Belgium, it has been more marked – from forty-five per cent in 1964 to thirty-four per cent in 1972.[26] The West German figures are similar – from forty-six per cent in 1960 to thirty-three per cent in 1973.[27] The most precipitate decline has been in the Netherlands, where the official church attendance figures dropped from sixty-four per cent in 1966 (when the series begins) to twenty-six per cent in 1979.[28] In France, no global figures are available, but Julien Potel has collated a number of local studies. While population shifts sometimes make precise comparisons difficult, the impression left by his data is of an almost universal decline in practice.[29] True, too much should not be read into these figures. It may be that, when a Catholic today ceases to practise his religion regularly, this implies a less absolute break with his Church than it would have done in the days before Vatican II, when more rigorous norms were accepted. Even when such qualifications are made, there can be little doubt that such figures show some kind of decline in the commitment which many Catholics feel for their Church. Here must be an important reason for the fact, already noted, that during the sixties and early seventies Catholic parties and social organisations were becoming either less powerful or less confessional, or both.

In the middle and later seventies, there have been signs that the decline of closed Catholicism has slowed. The abortion issue has, despite the German bishops' disappointment in 1972, on the whole proved one on which Catholics of otherwise divergent views can unite. The disenchantment with Catholic education, which so marked the late sixties and early seventies, seems to have died away. The general mood of contention and self-questioning which the Second Vatican Council called forth has become less evident. The decline of Christian Democratic parties has in most countries been halted or even reversed. The German Christian Democrats in 1976 were up by four per cent of the vote on their performance in 1972, although they lost ground again in 1980. The Belgian Christian Socials had by 1977 regained almost six per cent of the vote, as compared with their post-war nadir in 1971. The Dutch Catholic party responded to its debacle in 1972 by forming a federation with the two main Protestant parties; and the joint performance of the new formation, Christian Democratic Appeal, in the general election of 1977 suggested that the decline had been contained. The Swiss and Italian Christian Democrats have on the whole held their own. Only the Austrian Christian Democrats have continued, though gently, to decline.

These facts, however, do not contradict the underlying trend. Recent successes by Christian Democratic parties are interpreted by their historian, R.E.M. Irving, as the result of skilful adaptation by their leadership to changed circumstances, rather than to any favourable turn in the circumstances themselves.[30] They may also be connected with a general swing to the right that some observers have detected in western electorates. On the whole, the factors which produced a strong closed Catholicism in continental Europe have permanently passed away, and a reaction towards closed Catholicism is unlikely.

In the Anglo-American world, most of the factors operative in continental Europe have also been at work. True, there was little sign that socialist or liberal parties were 'de-anti-clericalising' themselves, because they had not been anti-clerical in the first place; but the decline in the distinctiveness of Catholic social teaching was just as evident to Anglo-American Catholics as it was to continental Europeans. A left-wing minority – such as the Berrigan brothers in the United States – has been just as vocal. The ferment caused by the Second Vatican Council was just as strongly felt. There was at least as much questioning of the traditional Catholic policy on education among English-speaking Catholics as there was in continental Europe. In the United States, a book published in 1964, Mary Perkins Ryan's *Are Parochial Schools the Answer?*, provoked a long-running controversy. In Australia, New Zealand, England and Scotland, similar controversies began at about the same date,[31] and in Ireland a little later. Curiously, this self-questioning on the Catholic side has come at a time when governments have shown themselves increasingly willing to meet the traditional Catholic demands. In Australia, state and federal governments began during the nineteen-sixties to reverse a ninety-year-old tradition, by giving financial aid to Catholic schools. In England, the rate of aid to Catholic schools was increased in 1959 and again in 1966. Even in the United States, where the Supreme Court has ruled that direct aid to parochial schools would be unconstitutional, indirect means of support such as the provision of textbooks or transport have become widespread.

Anglo-American Catholicism has been suffering the same erosion of its demographic base as Catholicism in continental Europe. Two sociological studies of American Catholicism, undertaken in 1963 and 1973, showed a decline in practice rate during the period from seventy-one per cent to fifty per cent.[32] In England and Wales, official figures showed that the number of Catholics at mass on the first Sunday in May each year dropped from 2,114,214 in 1966 to 1,831,550 in 1973.[33] In Australia, Gallup poll data indicated an over-all decline of Sunday churchgoing in the period 1961–72 from forty-four per cent to thirty-one per cent, to which Catholics contributed disproportionately.[34] In Canada, one set of polls showed the percentage of Catholics claiming to have attended church weekly as dropping from eighty-three in 1965 to fifty-nine in 1974, while another set showed the decline over the same period as being from seventy-nine to forty-nine.[35] Only in Ireland is there no evidence of much decline in religious practice. There, a number of surveys in the seventies indicated a practice rate of more than ninety per cent.[36]

In the English-speaking world there may be a further influence reducing Catholic unity which is not evident in continental Europe. This is the growing social mobility of Catholics. In the nineteenth and well into the twentieth centuries, Catholics in English-speaking countries seem to have been disproportionately concentrated in the working classes. This gave them a double reason for perceiving themselves as an outgroup and strengthened their group solidarity. Recent data suggest that in some of these countries this characteristic has declined or disappeared. In Australia, census figures show that the occupational profile of Catholics is now not far from that of the population as a whole.[37] In the United States, there is evidence to show that the income level of the average Catholic is now actually higher than that of the average Protestant.[38] In Britain, statistical evidence is harder to come by, but the impression of many observers is that the Catholic middle class has increased since the Second World War. As Catholics become more dispersed among different social classes, it would not be surprising if they came to behave less as a bloc politically.

For all these reasons, there has been a shift among Anglo-American Catholics towards the open end of the spectrum. The shift has been less dramatic than in continental Europe, because Anglo-American Catholics were much nearer that end of the spectrum already, but it is detectable. Among social organisations, many have de-confessionalised themselves or disappeared altogether. In Canada, the Catholic trade unions secularised themselves in 1960. In Britain and the United States, the Associations of Catholic Trade Unionists appear to be moribund. In England, the Catholic Social Guild has been wound up. In Ireland, the Catholic Workers' College has been renamed the College of Industrial Relations. In Australia, the Movement – the once-celebrated Catholic ginger group within the trade unions – ceased during the sixties to have any importance.

In their choice of political party, Anglo-American Catholics have moved even further from the closed position than they were in the nineteen-fifties. In Australia, the Democratic Labor party declined steadily in importance, as the issues which had brought it into existence faded into history, until at the general election of 1977 it put up candidates in only one state (Victoria). In Quebec, the *Union nationale*, which had once successfully projected itself as the defender of Catholic social teaching, was defeated by the Liberals in 1960, at a provincial general election in which the Church seems generally to have been neutral. After a last period of office in 1966–70, it has now declined to the status of a minor party. The gap left in provincial politics by its decline has been filled by the meteoric rise of a new party, the *Parti québécois*. The issue between the *Parti québécois* and the Liberal party is independence for the province of Quebec, which the former demands and the latter opposes. In this contest, religious issues appear to have no place. So far as I can discover from the secondary literature, neither party has a greater appeal to practising Catholics than the other. Elsewhere, the old generalisation that Catholics vote for the more left-wing of the two major parties – a fact which indicated at least a measure of Catholic political unity – may be losing part of its force. Survey data in Australia indicate that the Liberal and Country parties have since the fifties been picking up an increasing proportion of the Catholic vote.[39] In Canadian national elections, surveys still indicate a strong link between being a Catholic and voting Liberal; but one recent piece of research suggests that this is a matter of family inheritance rather than of reaction to any current political issue.[40] This seems a fragile base for its continuance.

In the United States, the sixties began with what might appear as a regression towards closed Catholicism. In the presidential election of 1960, there was a greater concentration of Catholics behind one party than at any time since survey data became available.[41] There was, however, a special reason for this: the Democrats were running a Catholic, John

F. Kennedy, as their candidate. This was the first time that a Catholic had stood for the presidency with a real chance of winning, and many Catholics who might not otherwise have voted Democrat seem to have been attracted by the prospect of putting 'one of their own' into the highest office in the country. On the other hand, some Protestants and agnostics who might otherwise have voted Democrat seem to have been deterred from doing so by the candidate's Catholicism. Kennedy's victory – even though by a hair's breadth margin in the popular vote – seems to have defused this issue permanently. Since 1960, there is some evidence of a slow decline in the identification between Catholics and the Democratic party.[42]

The bishops of the Anglo-American world, like those of continental Europe, appear to have grown more cautious about attempting to guide the political behaviour of their flocks. Whereas in the nineteen-forties the Boston clergy actively opposed an attempt to relax the Massachusetts law on birth control, in the nineteen-sixties Cardinal Cushing did not oppose change, and the law was amended.[43] Where bishops have tried to provide guidance, they have not always been able to bring the faithful with them. An American Jesuit has given examples from his own country: 'Catholics testified in favor of the liberalization of New York's adultery-only statute, despite the pressure of the bishops to retain a measure the effectuation of which was attended by widespread, suborned perjury. Catholics similarly testified before a Senate committee as to the legitimacy of the Federal government making birth control information available at home and abroad, while the Archbishop of Washington and the Apostolic Delegate were damning the government's action.'[44]

In so far as bishops do speak, they seem now, like their brethren in continental Europe, to have widened their horizons from protecting the interests of the Church to making judgments on the wider society. In the early seventies, the American bishops set new precedents for themselves when they supported a boycott called by exploited Mexican-American workers, and when they condemned (admittedly at a late stage in the conflict) the Vietnam War as unjust.[45] Even the Irish hierarchy, in some ways still a conservative body, can on social issues now be described as a centre-left critic of Irish society, calling for a more equal distribution of wealth or for greater aid to the Third World.[46]

Thus by the beginning of the nineteen-eighties, the wheel is coming full circle. Catholics in continental Europe and those in the Anglo-American world are closer together in their political behaviour than they have been at any time since the eighteen-forties. Both are moving nearer the open end of the spectrum. In both groups of countries, Catholic parties and social organisations are declining, de-confessionalising themselves, or both. Episcopal guidance to the electorate is less frequent and more cautiously phrased than it used to be. There is a greater diversity of political opinion. Instead of being clustered disproportionately towards either the centre-right (as in continental Europe) or the centre-left (as in the Anglo-American world), Catholics seem to be more evenly spread across the left-wing voting in Anglo-America at the very time when left-wing views have become increasingly fashionable among some Catholics in continental Europe. There is still some way to go before Catholic political behaviour is similar in the two groups of countries, but convergence is occurring – and it is occurring nearer to the position which Anglo-American Catholics have held. The gap which opened up in the second half of the nineteenth century between the Catholics of continental Europe and those of Anglo-America seems at last to be closing.

6

Conclusions and implications

The main conclusions which can be drawn out of the preceding discussion are as follows:

1. There are important variations over space in the political behaviour of Catholics in western democracies. The most striking difference is between continental Europe, which is the heartland of closed Catholicism and the Anglo-American world, which is the stronghold of open Catholicism. There are differences within each group of countries, but in most respects these are less than the differences between them.

   Various reasons for the contrast between continental Europe and Anglo-America can be suggested. The following appear to have weight:

   (a) It has been partly a question of proportionate strength. In the Anglo-American world, Catholics have been either very strong (Ireland, Quebec) and so have not needed a closed organisation, or rather weak (USA, Australia, English Canada, Britain, New Zealand) and so would not have profited from a closed organisation. In continental Europe, on the other hand, Catholics have been in an intermediate band of strength, strong enough for a closed Catholicism to be practicable and weak enough for it to be desirable. However, this cannot be the whole explanation. Though an appropriate balance of numbers seems to be a necessary condition for a closed Catholicism to arise, it is not a sufficient condition. A closed Catholicism does not arise everywhere that numbers are sufficient to support it.

   (b) The difference in Catholic political behaviour between the two groups of countries seems to reflect differences in the wider political culture. Anglo-

American countries in general seem to be less sharply divided into sub-cultures than those of continental Europe. Fully to explain the difference in *Catholic* political behaviour between the two groups of countries, then, it would be desirable to have a theory which explains the differences in their overall political behaviour. No such theory appears to be available. However, even in the absence of such a theory it has proved possible to offer a tolerably complete explanation of the divergence in Catholic political activity between the two groups of countries.

(c) The crucial cause of the divergence in Catholic political behaviour between the two groups of countries seems to have arisen at a particular period in the nineteenth century. Roughly in the years 1850–70, Catholics in continental Europe found themselves responding to what they saw as liberal aggression, by making a pan-conservative alliance with other right-wing forces. This alliance proved electorally unprofitable, and closed Catholicism largely grew out of the efforts of Catholics to distance themselves from these unpopular allies. In the Anglo-American world, on the other hand, Catholics, far from being prime targets for liberals, were their electoral allies. This alliance did not prove disadvantageous, and was maintained.

2. However, variations over space have been less important than variations over time. Though there is a contrast between continental Europe and Anglo-America, it has been at its maximum for a relatively brief period of time. Before about 1870, open Catholicism was the norm in both groups of countries. Since about 1960, Catholics in both groups of countries have been converging near the open end of the spectrum. Even in the years when the contrast was its greatest, the direction of movement in both groups of countries was the same. In both, Catholics were tending towards the closed end of the spectrum. The difference was that they moved further in continental Europe.

3. From the two generalisations listed above it follows that open Catholicism is a more widespread phenomenon than closed Catholicism. This is probably because it is a wider

concept, covering a greater variety of situations. A Catholicism may be described as 'open' in either of the following circumstances:

(a) Where political mobilisation has not yet taken place, and politics is the preserve of a small elite who do not require the backing of mass organisations. This was true of all the countries examined in this book, except the United States, until quite late in the nineteenth century.

(b) Where political mobilisation has taken place and participation is high, but where it has not taken place on confessional lines. There are two main factors which may inhibit mobilisation on confessional lines:
   (i) The balance of numbers may be inappropriate. Where Catholics are either very strong or very weak, a closed Catholicism will be either unnecessary or unprofitable. This is true of most parts of the Anglo-American world.
   (ii) Confessionally-related issues are not salient in politics. This has on the whole been true in the Anglo-American world. It is becoming true of continental Europe.

On the other hand, closed Catholicism is a more sharply-defined phenomenon. It means that Catholics have organised themselves with their own party and social organisations and under strong clerical guidance in an insulated sub-culture within the larger polity. For this to happen, the following conditions must be fulfilled:

(a) Political mobilisation must have ocurred. Hence the absence of more than preliminary signs of a closed Catholicism anywhere in Europe before about 1870.

(b) Political mobilisation must have occurred along confessional lines. For this to have happened, two further conditions must have been fulfilled:
   (i) The balance of numbers must be appropriate. Catholics must be few enough for separate organisations to seem necessary, but numerous enough for it to seem profitable.
   (ii) Confessional issues must have been salient at the time political mobilisation was taking place.

This is a restrictive set of conditions. They have been met in only some of the countries discussed in this book – those of continental Europe – and then only for a particular period, roughly 1870–1960.

4. It is not surprising, then, that closed Catholicism should be a rarer phenomenon than open Catholicism. It would be wrong, however, to go to the other extreme, and imply that a totally open Catholicism – i.e. a situation in which there was no difference between the political behaviour of Catholics and that of other citizens – was normal. For that to happen, one of the following conditions would have to obtain:
   (a) There must be no issues whatever dividing Catholics from their fellow-citizens. History suggests that this is unlikely to happen. Even as one issue subsides, such as education, another may arise, such as abortion, on which Catholics and others tend to have different preferences. Even if there is no religiously-related *issue* active, there may be an effect from religiously-related *status differences.*[1] Catholics may either feel resentment because they appear to be of lower status or provoke resentment because they appear to be of higher status.
   (b) All political parties (and social organisations) must be equidistant from the Catholic position, so that Catholics receive no advantage from supporting one party or organisation rather than another. Such a position of equilibrium is not impossible, but in practice it is hard to think of cases where it has occurred. If a distinctive Catholic interest exists, one party has always been perceived as more sympathetic to that interest than its competitors, and thus has tended to pick up the Catholic vote.

   Thus, though it is common for Catholics to be nearer the open end of the spectrum than the closed end, it is unusual for them to be right at the open end. In arithmetical terms one might suggest that the commonest position for Catholics to occupy is about three-quarters of the way towards the open end of the spectrum.

5. Next, a word about the position of Catholics on the left-right spectrum. Discussion so far has centred round varia-

tions in the position of Catholics on the closed-open axis. However, in preceding chapters a fair amount of information has been offered *en passant* about the position of Catholics on the left-right axis, and it is time to bring this information together.

There is no simple correlation between positions on the two axes. While the open Catholicism of the Anglo-American countries has generally been a left-wing one, it does not follow that the closed Catholicism of continental Europe has generally been a right-wing one. On the contrary, Catholics in continental Europe have tended to be most right-wing when they have been relatively open. This was evident in the generation 1850–70, when an open Catholicism of the right developed on the continent at the same time as an open Catholicism of the left prevailed in the Anglo-American world. It was detectable also in the inter-war years, when the appeal of fascism pulled many Catholics to the right – but in doing so undermined closed Catholicism. On the other hand, the two great growth periods of closed Catholicism – the period leading up to about 1920 and again the period after the Second World War – were accompanied by a reaction against right-wing alliances which had proved politically unprofitable or morally distasteful. Thus, closed Catholicism can perhaps best be pictured as a force of the centre. Open Catholicism may take three forms:

(a) an open Catholicism of the right – as in continental Europe before 1870, or to a lesser extent in the period 1920–40

(b) an open Catholicism of the left – as generally in the Anglo-American world

(c) a dispersed open Catholicism, in which Catholics are distributed fairly evenly along the left-right spectrum. This dispersed open Catholicism has perhaps never existed in a pure form anywhere, but approximations to it could be found in Europe before about 1850; and both continental Europe and Anglo-America seem to be moving towards it today.

Once again, closed Catholicism appears as a more sharply-defined phenomenon than open Catholicism. It is associated with one point on the closed-open axis; open Catholicism can be associated with three different positions.

6. It is now time to see if the preceding conclusions can be pulled together into one general model of Catholic political behavior. Table 3 is an attempt to summarise the findings so far. The main point to emerge is that Catholics in

Table 3. Catholic political behaviour 1820–1960

	Continental Europe		Anglo-American countries	
	Position on:		Position on:	
Period	Open-closed axis	Left-right axis	Open-closed axis	Left-right axis
1820–50	open	dispersed – right is stronger in some countries but left in others	open	tending to left
1850–70	open	moving to right	open	ditto
1870–1920	becoming closed	moving *from* right to centre	open – but some signs of closure	ditto
1920–60	some reaction towards open in first half of period, but generally closed	some movement to right in first half of period, but generally central	open – but some signs of closure	ditto
1960–	moving towards open	becoming more dispersed – considerable left-wing minority	open	dispersed – becoming less identified with left

continental Europe have described a great arc, from an open Catholicism well dispersed along the left-right axis, to a closed Catholicism bunched in the centre, to once again an open Catholicism dispersed along the left-right axis. Among Anglo-American Catholics this arc is much less evident, but it is detectable.

It could be argued that this 'normal curve' of Catholic development is not just the product of historical accident, but is a natural response by an ancient and conservative institution such as the Catholic Church to the rapid social change of the last hundred and thirty years. It has four main components:

(a) An open Catholicism bunches on the right in the period 1850–70. This marked an understandable effort by Catholics, faced with a liberal offensive, to find allies among other conservatives.
(b) This alliance, however, proves unprofitable. Catholics distance themselves from conservative allies and in doing so stress their unity as Catholics. Closed Catholicism emerges, less right-wing than the preceding open Catholicism.
(c) This closed centrist Catholicism burgeons in the period 1870–1960.
(d) The circumstances which fostered the growth of closed Catholicism die away. It consequently becomes possible for Catholics to move to a more open position along the open-closed axis, and to disperse themselves along the left-right axis.

This 'normal curve' is less visible among Anglo-American Catholics because the circumstances which caused it in Europe were less applicable. Anglo-American Catholics never felt the need for the pan-conservative alliance in the later nineteenth century from which, in Europe, the whole cycle started. At the same time, they could not help being aware of and influenced by what their European co-religionists were doing. The behaviour of Anglo-American Catholics, then, was the resultant of two forces: the needs of their own situation and developments in the wider Catholic Church. The result was that they followed the 'normal curve' less decisively than Catholics in continental Europe, but they followed it none the less.

The concept of a normal curve of Catholic development over the last century and a quarter – followed more vigorously in some countries than others, but detectable in all – is, it may be suggested, the most important conclusion to emerge from this study.

In the final section of this chapter I should like to draw out some possible implications of the preceding argument. In the introduction, I expressed the hope that this study might be of interest to workers in three different fields: the history of Catholicism in particular countries, the comparative study of political cleavages, and the sociology of religion. I should like now to suggest some possible implications of my findings for these three areas.

1. *The history of Catholicism in particular countries.* One advantage of a general theory, such as the one suggested in this book is that it draws attention to questions which might otherwise not be asked. For instance, if the preceding account is correct, a fact which needs explaining is the growing divergence in the late nineteenth century between the Catholics of continental Europe and those of Anglo-America. One group became the pioneers of closed Catholicism, while the other remained closer to open Catholicism. In Chapter 3, I suggested some explanations for this divergence. But how far are they accurate? Even if accurate enough in general, do they require amendment for particular countries?

   Perhaps it is the behaviour of Catholics in the Anglo-American countries which most needs investigation. Historians of Catholicism in continental Europe cannot help noticing the rise of closed Catholicism, even if they do not use the term, and most books touching on the period contain some discussion of the development. However, it is easy for a historian of an Anglo-American country to overlook the fact that closed Catholicism did not arise there. Historians tend to concentrate on explaining what did happen and take for granted what did not happen. For instance, I do not know of anyone who has worked on nineteenth-century Ireland – including myself – to whom it has occurred to ask: why did Ireland *not* throw up a Catholic party, Catholic trade unions, or Catholic farmers' organisations? Yet, at a period when such parties and organisations were developing in many parts of Europe, their absence is striking enough to deserve examination. The same applies to other Anglo-American countries.

Again, the convergence between the two groups of countries after 1960 deserves further investigation. The general picture – the decline of distinctively Catholic organisations, the dispersal of the Catholic vote – is not in question. Studies of particular countries in this period have often stressed such features. What a comparative study such as this can do is to bring out factors which, in a study confined to one country, might not be so apparent. For instance, in the preceding chapter some stress was put on the declining distinctiveness of Catholic social teaching. Was this indeed an important feature? Can its influence be traced in the study of particular countries?

This work has brought out one gap in the literature – the relative absence of studies of clerical influence in politics. The definitions of closed and open Catholicism used in this book have three components: the degree to which Catholics maintain political parties of their own; the degree to which they form social organisations of their own; and the degree to which they act under the political guidance of their clergy. For the first two components, the literature presented no great difficulties; histories exist of nearly all the major parties and social organisations, Catholic or other. The third component was much harder to cover. Studies of the political activity and influence of the bishops and lower clergy in different countries are regrettably rare. Yet in any comprehensive survey of Catholic political behaviour, it is as important to cover this aspect as it is to cover the history of the formal organisations.

Finally, this work may have implications for the study of countries outside the thirteen selected for investigation here. How do Spain, Portugal, eastern Europe, the various states of Latin America, fit in – at least for those periods when they could be classified as liberal democracies? My impression is that Catholics in those countries have tended to follow the same curve as Catholics in continental Europe, but in a less pronounced manner – perhaps because a lower level of economic development has brought with it a lower level of political development, whether Catholic or other – but this is a matter for investigation. So is the wider question, of whether the closed-open classification has any relevance for the study of Catholics in authoritarian countries.

2. *The comparative study of political cleavages.* One generalisation to emerge from recent work on political cleavages is that the cleavages which happened to be dominant at quite an early stage in a country's history – at or even before the period of mass mobilisation – have a crucial importance for its subsequent political development. As Lipset and Rokkan put it in their study of the development of party systems in western Europe: 'the decisive sequence of party formation took place at the early stage of competitive politics, in some cases well before the extension of the franchise, in other cases on the very eve of the rush to mobilize the finally enfranchised masses.'[2]

   The findings of this study support their view. Where the division between Catholics and others was important during the period of mass mobilisation in the late nineteenth century, it has continued to be important down to the present, even if in recent years its significance has at last begun to decline. Where the division between Catholics and others was not the most salient at the time of mass mobilisation, it has remained less important since.

   However, this study goes a stage further, and discusses how and why the cleavage between Catholics and others proved to be so important. In continental Europe, the crucial factors seem to lie in the generation 1850–70. It was then that continental liberals became increasingly militant, and that Catholics increasingly took refuge in a pan-conservative alliance. After 1870, the drawbacks to this pan-conservative alliance became apparent, and Catholics tried to distance themselves from it by organising on a more progressive – but also more confessional – basis.

Now if this is true, it goes a long way towards explaining why cleavages in late-nineteenth-century Europe took the form they did, but it does not offer a complete explanation. For the Catholic sub-cultures were not the only ones that were crystallising out in that region and period: there were also socialist sub-cultures and in the Netherlands a Calvinist one. The complexity shown by some of these fully equalled that of any Catholic sub-culture. The German Social Democrats, for instance, had tight links with the major trade-union federation, and were also 'surrounded by a network of affiliated associations, such as youth organisations, sports clubs, dramatic and literary associations, glee clubs and organisations for the spread of atheism. It was fitting to say that in his work and leisure the Social Democratic worker was organised "from the cradle to the grave".'[3] The Dutch Calvinist sub-culture can be explained in terms similar to the Catholic ones, for it too arose in conscious reaction against the liberal hegemony. The very name of its political arm – the Anti-Revolutionary party – proclaimed its repudiation of the principles of the Revolution of 1789. The socialist sub-cultures require a different explanation. They were not so much a repudiation of liberalism, as a development of it. What needs to be investigated is why a group with such different antecedents from the Catholics should have developed in similar ways. The general histories of socialism are of surprisingly little help here. Though such histories abound, they are primarily histories of socialist thought, not of socialist organisation. Even studies of socialism in individual countries rarely concentrate on the development of the sub-culture – Guenther Roth's *The Social Democrats in Imperial Germany* is one of the few exceptions. Perhaps, by studying Catholic developments in continental Europe during these years, we have drawn attention to a gap in the literature on socialist developments. A study of the rise of closed Catholicism needs to be complemented by a study of the rise of closed socialism.

3. *The sociology of religion*. As was pointed out in the introduction, the comparative study of different types of Catholicism has been surprisingly neglected by soci-

ologists. Yet there is certainly a field for investigation. Perhaps this work by a political scientist can act as trail-blazer.

The questions which I hope it may raise for sociologists are as follows. Supposing the picture given here of variations in the political behaviour of Catholics is accurate, how far is it paralleled by variations in the behaviour of Catholics in other areas? Do the same variations over space and over time recur in forms of piety, levels of practice, forms of apostolate, levels of scholarship? Or do different patterns reveal themselves in different fields? For instance, the concepts of 'closed' and 'open' Catholicism could be extended to other spheres of life besides those studied in this book. In some countries, the Church has been more successful than in others in building up a self-contained education system or a comprehensive Catholic press. In some it has been more insistent than in others on discouraging mixed marriages. If these variations were to be studied, they might turn out to be distributed rather differently from the variations between 'closed' and 'open' Catholicism in the political field. On the other hand, in the history of Catholic scholarship one can perhaps detect a normal curve such as can be discerned in the history of Catholic political behaviour – from a relative openness in the early nineteenth century, through a peak of closedness at the time of the modernist crisis in the early twentieth century, to another period of relative openness in the late twentieth century. All these similarities and differences deserve to be plotted and explained.

In a survey such as this, which seeks to cover thirteen countries in sixty thousand words, only the main lines of development can be traced. To every generalisation I have made there are exceptions. Many of these I am aware of; others will doubtless have escaped me. Since I cannot possibly be authoritative on all thirteen countries, there are bound to be errors of fact as well.

I hope, however, that such errors and oversimplifications will not be so serious as to vitiate the purpose of the book. That purpose has been to develop a hitherto neglected area of scholarship – the study of variations within Catholicism. I have argued that the subject deserves more attention from historians, political scientists and sociologists than it has received. I have attempted to open up the field in three ways:

1. by suggesting a pair of ideal types, 'open' and 'closed' Catholicism, which can be used to classify differences in the political behaviour of Catholics;
2. by describing variations in Catholic political behaviour, over space and over time, in terms of those ideal types;
3. by offering explanations for the variations which emerge.

I do not imagine that my presentation under any of these headings will prove definitive, but if I have provided a starting-point for further investigation, that will be sufficient accomplishment.

APPENDIX A

The Vallier typology

So far as I can discover the only previous social scientist to have attempted to develop a typology of Catholicism is a sociologist specialising on Latin America, the late Ivan Vallier. It is worth examining Vallier's schema to see how far it meshes with the conclusions arrived at in this book. His typology can be found in two places: in Chapter IV of his book *Catholicism, Social Control, and Modernization in Latin America* (Englewood Cliffs, 1970), and in a paper, 'Extraction, insulation and re-entry: toward a theory of religious change', published in a volume edited by Henry Landsberger, *The Church and Social Change in Latin America* (Notre Dame, 1970). I shall for preference use the latter formulation, which is more succinct, and leaves the impression of having been written later.[1]

Vallier sees the Latin American Church as having evolved through five stages:

1. *The monopoly Church* – territorial dominance and legal privilege. The Church has great influence, through its control of the education system, through privileged access to secular rulers, and through a legal monopoly which protects it from competition. However, it is strictly controlled by the state, and its clergy are essentially civil bureaucrats. This stage corresponds most closely with colonial times, though in some countries it lasted long after that.
2. *The political Church* – short-run coalitions and clerical threats. As liberal forces gain strength, the Church experiences sharp curtailments of its privileges. Churchmen counter by moving to the side of the conservatives, which inevitably draws the Church into partisan conflicts.

This stage was at its most fully developed in the second half of the nineteenth century.

3. *The ghetto Church* – insulation and offence. Church leaders come to recognise the disadvantages of the conservative coalitions favoured in stage 2, which alienate many of the laity. They move instead to 'a strategy of influence that combines confessionalism with the establishment of specialized structures that are to insulate Catholicism from secular forces.'[2] This is the period of organised Catholic Action and of specialised Catholic groups such as trade unions, youth groups, schools, charities and welfare programmes. In Chile, Brazil and Argentina, this stage can be traced back to the second and third decades of the twentieth century, though elsewhere it started later or has never really developed.
4. *The servant Church* – social development and institution-building. This stage marks a change from a defensive and antagonistic relation to society, to an acceptance of responsibility for facilitating social goals. The Church throws itself into programmes for the betterment of society. Direct political battles are avoided, even though the programmes adopted imply a progressive political position. This stage began, particularly in Brazil, Chile and Colombia, in the early nineteen-sixties.
5. *The pastoral Church* – religious leadership and congregational forms. The Church now begins to grow beyond even the social and economic programmes favoured in the preceding stage. The bishop becomes above all a teacher, concerning to bring home to the faithful their social responsibilities. The priest becomes a community leader, aiming to develop his congregation as human beings, without infringing on their individual autonomy. This stage could be detected as just beginning in the late nineteen-sixties.

Although Vallier does not employ the terms 'left' and 'right', or 'closed' and 'open', his typology can be reformulated in these terms. I have attempted such a reformulation in Table 4. When Table 4 is compared with the left-hand side of Table 3 above, it brings out similarities between the developments which Vallier has detected in Latin America, and those which I have detected in continental Europe. Vallier's first stage, the monopoly Church, has indeed no parallel in my model, but a counterpart could easily be built in – the *ancien régime* in Europe had much the same characteristics. Vallier's second stage, the political Church, corresponds to the stage 1850–70 in continental Europe. His third stage, the ghetto Church, corresponds to my third and fourth stages, covering 1870–1960, in continental Europe, when closed Catholicism was flourishing. His fourth and fifth stages correspond to the fifth stage in continental Europe, covering the period since 1960, in which closed Catholicism has been declining. Indeed the similarities are so extensive that at one point I considered using the Vallier thesis as my starting-point, constructing this book as an answer to the question 'How well does the Vallier model fit other parts of the world besides Latin America?'.

Table 4.

Stage	Position on:	
	Open-closed axis	Left-right axis
1. The monopoly Church	n.a. – distinction had not yet arisen	n.a. – distinction had not yet arisen
2. The political Church	open	right
3. The ghetto Church	closed	centre
4. The servant Church	more open	tending to left
5. The pastoral Church	open	tending to left

However, enough weaknesses exist in the Vallier typology for this to be impracticable. There were a number of points where reformulation seemed desirable before one could even begin to apply it elsewhere, and by the time these reformulations had been built in, one would no longer be testing the Vallier model. Indeed, after discussing the Vallier model with Latin American specialists, I have the impression that it needs reformulation even with respect to Latin America. A number of modifications seem to be required, which I shall put in ascending order of importance:

1. Vallier excludes from his model the Christian Democratic parties, which have arisen in a number of Latin American countries, even if they have never been quite so important as in continental Europe. They can in fact be fitted in easily – they are one more example of the insulation of Catholics during the third, or ghetto, stage – but they deserve a specific mention.
2. Vallier's last two stages might be collapsed into one. Certainly in Europe it is difficult to distinguish the two, and it may not be easy even in Latin America. Vallier acknowledges that they have arisen in quick succession and indeed overlap. It might be better to abandon the distinction and to categorise the strategies which he assigns to respectively the servant and the pastoral Church as alternative strategies employed during the same stage.
3. Vallier has no equivalent to my first stage, covering the period 1820–50 – a period which might be labeled the 'incipient liberal', in which a considerable proportion of Catholics experimented with the possibilities of a liberal alliance, and in which the identity of Catholicism and conservatism was not so apparent as it later became. Yet this period existed in Latin America as well as in continental Europe. While most bishops opposed the struggle for independence in the Latin American colonies, many priests and Catholic laymen supported it. In Mexico, the rebellion against Spanish rule was led by two priests. The early independent regimes, whether liberal or conservative, all agreed in confirming the privileges of the Catholic Church. It was only from mid-century on that liberals became increasingly anti-clerical and that committed Catholics became increasingly conservative. It is important to build the 'incipient liberal' stage into the model, because it shows that the transition to conservatism was not inevitable, and suggests that, if things had turned out differently, a leap to the final stage might have occurred a century earlier than it has actually done.
4. In one formulation of his model – that presented in the volume edited by Landsberger – Vallier stresses that the Church *withdraws* from the world. Indeed he subtitles this presentation of his thesis 'extraction-insulation-re-entry',

with the insulation occurring in the third stage, and the re-entry occurring in the fourth. This seems to give a misleading picture of what the Church was doing in this stage. It is doubtful that it was any more withdrawn from the world then than it was either earlier or later. All that differed was the method by which it sought to act on the world. This seems to be true in Latin America as well as in continental Europe. The concepts of insulation and withdrawal are better left out of the model.

For all these reasons I decided that it was not practicable to apply the Vallier model as it stood. I am, however, encouraged by the fact that a scholar starting from quite different considerations – Vallier was interested in the practical problem of how to encourage the Church to take a progressive and not a conservative line – and drawing his material from a quite different set of countries, should none the less have developed a model with so many similarities to my own.

APPENDIX B

Statistics of religious practice about 1960

In this appendix, I attempt to provide a rough estimate of the proportion of practising Catholics in the population of the thirteen countries which have been studied in depth in this book. The date to which the figures relate is about 1960. There are two reasons for this choice of date. First, I did not want to go any later because I wanted to choose a point before the decline of recent years in religious practice had gathered momentum. Second, I found it impracticable to go any earlier because the data were not available. In most countries, data on religious practice were not accumulated before the late fifties. In a few cases, such information as can be found comes from an even later date, and I have had to extrapolate backwards in order to arrive at an estimate for 1960.

There are many difficulties in interpreting data on religious practice. It would be as well to outline these before examining the figures. To arrive at an estimate of the proportion of practising Catholics in a given country, we first need two other figures: the proportion of nominal Catholics in the country and the proportion of practising Catholics among nominal Catholics. A word must be said about each.

1. *The proportion of nominal Catholics in each country.* In eight of the thirteen countries, this figure can be obtained from the census. In five countries – Belgium, France, Italy, Britain and the United States – no census figures are available, so we have to rely on data from other sources, such as ecclesiastical statistics of baptised Catholics or religious affiliation as recorded in opinion polls.
2. *The proportion of practising Catholics among nominal Catholics.* This is where the problems really accumulate. First, there is the question of definition: what does one mean by a

practising Catholic? Canon law lays the following obligations on Catholics:

(a) to attend mass every Sunday.

(b) to go to communion at least once a year, in a period of about two months centred round Easter. (In actuality, most practising Catholics go to communion considerably more often.)

(c) to go to confession at least once a year.[1] (Canon law does not state that this annual confession must be in the Easter period, but in practice those who go only annually to confession are likely to do so at the same time as their Easter communion.)

French sociologists of religion have invented two convenient terms to describe those who fulfill these obligations: *messalisant* and *pascalisant*. A *messalisant* is one who attends mass each Sunday, unless prevented by genuine cause. A *pascalisant* is one who goes to confession and communion at least once a year, and that in the period around Easter. A practising Catholic, then, is one who is both a *messalisant* and a *pascalisant*. To have a complete picture of the practice rate in a given country, then, we should have statistics for both categories. There are difficulties in collecting either of them.

Messalisants. There are two ways of finding out what proportion of Catholics attend Sunday mass – to ask them and to count them. Asking them is frequently done in public opinion surveys. In the case of Catholics, anyone claiming to go to church at least weekly can be considered as claiming to be a *messalisant*. The drawback to this method is that it seems to lead to exaggeration. More people claim in response to a survey question to attend church weekly than, it appears from other evidence, actually do so. Evidently, in countries such as those studied in this book, there is still an aura of respectability associated with church attendance. Some survey designers have tried to get round this difficulty by asking the more pointed question: 'Have you been to church within the last seven days?' The results have not been greatly different, and it seems that some respondents still claim to have attended church even when they have not done so.

The other way of estimating the proportion of *messalisants* is to start by counting the numbers present in church on a given

Sunday. The administrative arrangements for such a count can quite easily be made by the ecclesiastical authorities, and counts have been carried out on a diocesan or even a national scale in a number of countries. The problem then arises – what correction should be made for those unable to attend mass for a genuine reason? There are a number of good reasons which can keep the most conscientious Catholic away from church on a particular Sunday: sickness, the requirements of one's work, bad weather, distance from a church. Children under seven are also excused. Two of the leading French investigators, Boulard and Rémy, suggest that the numbers counted at mass on a given Sunday might need to be revised upwards by as much as fifty per cent to obtain a fair figure for *messalisants*.[2] Some of the data based on head-counts in church include a correction for those genuinely prevented from attending; but the basis for this correction varies between one investigation and another, and almost always seems to be too low.

Pascalisants. Here again, there are two ways of reaching a figure – by asking and by counting. Asking is rarely done: in only a handful of surveys have Catholic respondents been asked to state if they have fulfilled their Easter duty. Counting is more frequent and can be done as follows. As soon as the period for the fulfilment of the Easter duty begins, each priest starts counting the number of confessions he hears. One may ask how he manages to avoid double-counting those who go to confession more than once within the prescribed period. This is easily managed. Every time a Catholic goes to confession, he is supposed to state how long it is since his last confession. If his previous confession occurred since the period for the Easter duty began, the priest can omit him from the total. The main drawback to *pascalisant* figures is that they seem to exaggerate the number of practising Catholics. There appears to be, particularly in some parts of Europe, a significant number of Catholics who fulfil their Easter duties but who do not bother to go regularly to mass on Sundays.

Thus, none of the sources for statistics about religious practice is entirely satisfactory. Figures derived from surveys or from data on *pascalisants* are likely to be too high. Figures derived from church-attendance counts are likely to be too low. In the following discussion, I have described the nature of the data in each case and have tried to make the necessary corrections, but it must be emphasised that all estimates are only approximate. In many countries, the figures for the proportion of practising Catholics could easily be several per cent out.

THE DATA[3]

Continental Europe

A general point must be made about all the countries in this group: national figures are only averages, concealing marked differences between one region and another.

Austria

Nominal Catholics. The census of 1969 showed 89.0% of the population as Catholic.

Practising Catholics. Two studies are available, one by Erich Bodzenta and one by Paul Michael Zulehner, both drawing on official ecclesiastical statistics.[4] According to Bodzenta, the *messalisant* rate in 1958–60 was 34.5%, and the *pascalisant* rate was 46.5%. According to Zulehner, the *messalisant* rate in 1960 was 37.1%, and the *pascalisant* rate was 39.7%. Bodzenta states that he has corrected for those excused, but does not state exactly how he has done this. Zulehner says that he has gone on the assumption that 85% of nominal Catholics are obliged to attend mass on Sundays. Differences in the corrections made by the two authors may account for the difference in their percentage figures. In any case, the figures are close enough together to indicate roughly where the true practice rate must lie. I suggest 40% as the nearest round figure, while acknowledging that it may be on the high side.

Belgium

Nominal Catholics. There are no census data. However, Houtart – writing in the sixties – states (though without reference) that 96% of Belgians were baptised,[5] and we can take this as a provisional figure.

Practising Catholics. An ecclesiastical enquiry in 1950 put the proportion of *messalisants* at 49.6%, and another in 1962 put it at 46.1%.[6] A correction was made for those not obliged to attend, but it appears to have been too low, so one can suggest 50% as an approximate practice rate.

France

Nominal Catholics. There are no census data, but a nation-wide ecclesiastical enquiry in 1958 concluded that 91.4% of the population had been baptised in the Catholic faith.[7]

Practising Catholics. The best figures are provided by Boulard and Rémy, who, synthesising a mass of data collected by ecclesiastical authorities between 1952 and 1965, conclude that the *messalisant* rate was likely to be about 25–6%, and the *pascalisant* rate about 31–2%.[8] Since they are among the few writers to have corrected adequately for those excused from attendance, I propose to accept their *messalisant* figures as a reasonably accurate indicator of religious practice.

West Germany

Nominal Catholics. The census of 1961 showed 45.1% of the population (excluding West Berlin) as Catholics.

Practising Catholics. Annual figures are available from ecclesiastical sources. They show for 1960 (again excluding West Berlin) a *pascalisant* rate of 52.4% and a *messalisant* rate of 46.3%.[9] The figures are stated to be a percentage of the total Catholic population and would therefore appear to include no correction for those excused. One specialist writer, however, has stated that parish priests, when sending in their returns, have made a correction of about 15 per cent in the *messalisant* figures to cover such cases.[10] This suggests that only a modest further correction is required. The true figure, then, is likely to be between the official *pascalisant* figure (which, here as elsewhere, is likely to be on the high side) and the official *messalisant* figure, which is likely to be too low. We may suggest a figure of about 50%.

Italy

Nominal Catholics. No census data are available, nor, it seems, any ecclesiastical statistics about the proportions of Italians baptised. Since non-Catholic minorities are very small, and outright rejection of all religion seems rarer than in France, one can guess that the figure will be higher than the French one of 91.4%. I shall use 95% as a working estimate.

Practising Catholics. A poll in 1962 showed 53% of Italians as claiming to attend mass regularly. Burgalassi, conflating the results of counts made by ecclesiastical authorities in a large number of localities covering about 24% of the parishes in Italy, suggested a *messalisant* rate of 37% and a *pascalisant* rate of 61%.[11] Assuming that the true figure is somewhere in between, we can suggest a practice rate in the region of 45%. This is a very rough indication. The data for Italy are even more unsatisfactory than for most of the countries in this survey, and this estimate could easily be as much as 10% out.

The Netherlands

Nominal Catholics. The census of 1960 showed 40.4% of the population as Catholic.

Practising Catholics. An official source for 1960 gives a *pascalisant* rate of 87.7%.[12] Official *messalisant* figures do not become available until 1966, when they showed an average of 64.4% of the Catholic population aged seven years or over as attending mass on the two Sundays when the count was made.[13] This figure will require revision upwards before it can represent the situation in 1960 – partly because it takes no account of those excused for reasons other than age, partly because there are indications that the precipitate decline in practice which is so marked in contemporary Dutch Catholicism had already begun before 1966. A survey in 1956 found that 89% of Catholic respondents claimed to have attended mass during the preceding seven days.[14] Taking an intermediate figure, we can suggest a practice rate for 1960 of about 80%.

Switzerland

Nominal Catholics. The census of 1960 put Catholics at 45.4% of the population. However, in view of the number of foreigners in Switzerland with no voting rights, it is more relevant to take the proportion of Catholics among Swiss citizens. This came to 41.4%.

Practising Catholics. The data are poor for Switzerland. A national survey in 1962 produced a figure of 82% of Catholics claiming to go regularly to mass. This is too high to be credible. It is out of line with rates in neighbouring countries and also out of line with local enquiries in French-speaking Switzerland, which show a variety of rates from 85% in some rural areas to as low as 15% in some towns. A study published in 1961 is reported to have given a figure of 50%.[15] This is much more plausible and is the one that I shall adopt here.

Anglo-American countries

Australia

Nominal Catholics. The census of 1961 put Catholics at 24.9% of the population.

Practising Catholics. The data available all come from surveys. Polls in 1956 and 1960 found that 61% and 53% of Catholics claimed to have attended church in the previous seven days. Polls in 1961 and 1962 found 54% and 55% of Catholics claiming to attend mass every week.[16] In view of the tendency of surveys to exaggerate levels of practice, it might be prudent to adopt an estimate slightly lower than these figures. I therefore suggest a figure of 50% for Australia, while recognising that there is considerable room for error.

Canada

Nominal Catholics. The census of 1961 put Catholics at 45.7% of the population. In Quebec the figure was 88.1%; in the rest of Canada taken as a unit, 28.6%.

Practising Catholics. As in Australia, only survey data are available. Gallup polls found that, in 1956, 87% of Catholics claimed to have attended church in the preceding seven days and in 1965, 83%.[17] The Canadian election survey of 1965 found that 79% of Catholics claimed to attend mass once a week or more.[18] Taking the nearest round figure, one may suggest a practice rate of 80%.

In the Canadian case, it is important to provide figures for the different parts of the country. The election survey of 1965 is of value here: it found that 86% of Catholics in Quebec claimed to attend mass at least weekly and 68% of Catholics in the rest of the country. Again, taking a convenient round figure and remembering that surveys more often exaggerate than understate, one can suggest a practice rate of 85% for Quebec and 65% for the rest of Canada.

Ireland

Nominal Catholics. The census of 1961 put Catholics at 94.9% of the population.

Practising Catholics. Several national surveys in the seventies found practice rates in excess of 90%.[19] While surveys tend to exaggerate figures, practice rates are likely to have been even higher at the beginning of the sixties than they were later. The two factors may cancel each other out, and a practice rate of 90% is plausible for Ireland.

New Zealand

Nominal Catholics. The census of 1961 put Catholics at 14.9% of the population.

Practising Catholics. The data are scarcer for New Zealand than for any other country in this survey. Only two local surveys are available: a church-attendance count in Auckland in 1949, which found 75% of Catholics at mass, and a survey of Christchurch in 1962 which found that 68% of Catholics claimed to have been to church the previous Sunday. If these figures are accurate, they would suggest that the practice in New Zealand is higher than in Australia or Britain, the two countries it resembles most closely in other ways. I have not found anything in the general literature to suggest that this is true, and I therefore prefer to adopt a figure nearer to the British and Australian levels. I suggest 60%, but stress the tentative nature of the estimate.

United Kingdom

Although the United Kingdom of Great Britain and Northern Ireland is in international law one unit, the religious situation in its two components is so different that for practical purposes it is better to discuss them separately.

1. Great Britain

Nominal Catholics. The evidence from a large number of surveys, and from baptism and marriage statistics converges to suggest that about 11% of the population is nominally Catholic – rather more in Scotland, slightly less in England and Wales.

Practising Catholics. Two surveys in the fifties produced practice rates for Catholics of 44% and 52% respectively.[20] A survey in 1964 found 59% of Catholics claiming to go to mass twice or more per month,[21] so presumably the percentage claiming to go weekly would have been somewhat lower. An attendance count is available for England and Wales for 1960: it showed that 1,941,500 Catholics attended mass on the Sunday when the count was made.[22] The population of England and Wales in 1961 was 46,105,000. On the assumption that it was 10% Catholic, and making a correction for those excused attendance, this would indicate a practice rate of more than 50%. Taking a mean between these figures, we can suggest an estimate of very roughly 50%, while emphasising the unreliability of the figure.

2. Northern Ireland

Nominal Catholics. In this part of the United Kingdom, the census includes religious data. It put the proportion of Catholics in 1961 at 34.9%.

Practising Catholics. The earliest data came from a survey in 1968, which showed that 95% of Catholics claimed to go to church at least weekly.[23] This compares, as one might expect in view of the similar cultures of the Catholics in the two areas, with the figures for the Republic of Ireland. Allowing for a little exaggeration on the part of respondents, one might suggest a practice rate of 90%.

United States

Nominal Catholics. The decennial censuses in the United States do not collect data on religious affiliation. The Bureau of the Census does, however, make estimates of religious membership, and there are also figures available from opinion polls. These converge on a figure of about 25% as the proportion of Catholics in the United States around 1960.

Practising Catholics. Surveys provide the only data available. A poll in 1957 found 72% of Catholics claiming to go to mass at least once a week.[24] Another in 1963 produced a figure of 71%.[25] A poll in 1965 found 76% of Catholics claiming to have attended mass in the preceding seven days.[26] Allowing for some exaggeration, one might suggest a practice rate of 65%, similar to that for English-speaking Canada.

The figures arrived at in this appendix are summarised in Table 5. In conclusion, the tentative nature of these estimates must once again be stressed. The preceding discussion will have made clear the tenuous basis on which they rest in many countries. The figures, particularly in the middle column, may well be out by several percentage points.

Table 5. Summary: practice rates about 1960

	per cent of nominal Catholics in population	per cent of practising Catholics among nominal Catholics	per cent of practising Catholics in population
Continental Europe			
Austria	89	40	36
Belgium	96	50	48
France	91	25	23
West Germany	45	50	23
Italy	95	45	43
The Netherlands	40	80	32
Switzerland	41	50	21
Anglo-America			
Australia	25	50	13
Canada	46	80	37
Quebec	88	85	75
rest of Canada	29	65	19
Ireland	95	90	85
New Zealand	15	60	9
United Kingdom:			
Great Britain	11	50	6
Northern Ireland	35	90	32
United States	25	65	16

APPENDIX C

The case of Malta

Several people who read this work in draft asked why I had not discussed Malta. It would have been easy to reply that Malta is not usually included in the category of western democracies. Of the five authorities cited in footnote 1 to the Introduction, only one (Mackie and Rose's *International Almanac of Electoral History)* covers Malta. The others have excluded it, presumably either because it is much poorer than the typical western democracy, or because its experience of constitutional government has been too limited. Under British rule, it enjoyed responsible government, i.e. a ministry responsible to the elected legislature for all internal matters, only for brief and interrupted periods (1921–30, 1932–3, 1947–58, 1962–4). It has been an independent parliamentary democracy only since 1964.

However, to shelter behind considerations such as these would mean missing an opportunity to examine a theoretically interesting case. The significance of Malta lies in the fact that it does not easily fit into the closed-open classification.

In one respect, the political behaviour of Maltese Catholics has been fairly near the open end of the spectrum. Maltese Catholics have not formed a closed sub-culture, with their own party and social organisations, within the larger society. True, in the nineteen-sixties the Nationalist party emerged as the beneficiary of the clergy's good will, but this was a by-product of the latter's quarrel with the Labour party, which left them with no choice but implicitly to support the Nationalists as Labour's main rival. The Nationalist party, unlike the Christian Democratic parties of the continent, was not in origin a vehicle for Catholic social teaching. Social organisations, too, were not generally formed on a confessional base. The leading labour organisation, the General Workers' Union, though it was drawn into the Labour party's quarrel with the Church, was non-confessional in principle.[1] This perhaps was what one might expect. Though precise statistics are not available, a large majority of the Maltese population are practising Catholics. It would not be surprising, then, if – as in Ireland – no party or social organisation was specifically Catholic because all parties and social organisations had to take account of Catholic values.

In another respect, however, Malta lies on the extreme edge of closed Catholicism. This is shown in the unusual involvement in politics of the Maltese clergy on two occasions. The first was the quarrel with Lord Strickland, prime minister of Malta in 1927–32. The other was the running battle with Mr. Dom Mintoff, leader of the Malta Labour party, which continued through much of the nineteen-fifties and sixties and reached its peak in the general election of 1962. There is no necessity here to go into the reasons for these conflicts – though the leading historian of Maltese politics, Edith Dobie, indicates that both men provoked their quarrels with the Church.[2] Having been provoked, the Church went to lengths beyond those I have come across in any other country in the world.

One example was the denunciation of political opponents by name. This is unusual in church history. Even at the height of the Cold War, when hierarchies throughout continental Europe looked on Communists as irreconcilable enemies and Christian Democrats as the one sure bulwark against them, it was unusual for episcopal pastorals to denounce the Communist party, let alone individual Communist leaders, by name. Even if that was the clear import of a particular pastoral, it was left to the individual conscience to make the application.[3] The Maltese hierarchy, however, named not only parties but individuals. A pastoral letter issued before the general election of 1930 stated: 'You may not, without committing a grave sin, vote for Lord Strickland and his candidates, or for all those, even of other parties, who in the past have helped and supported him . . .'[4] Before the general election of 1962, the bishops laid an interdict on the members of Mintoff's party executive, while the clergy led a crusade of prayer and pilgrimage against a victory by Mintoff. These measures had some success. The general election of 1930 was suspended by the governor of Malta on the ground that it could not be free. The general election of 1962 proved a disappointment for Mintoff, since he gained only 34 per cent of the vote. He did not win a majority till 1971, by which time he had mended his quarrel with the Church.

Malta, then, is an anomalous case. My two ideal types, closed and open Catholicism, may be summarised as follows:

Closed	**Open**
1. All Catholics mobilised behind a Catholic political party.	1. Catholics divided between parties in the same manner as other citizens; no Catholic party.
2. All Catholics mobilised behind Catholic social organisations.	2. Catholics mobilised in the same social organisations as other citizens; no Catholic social organisations.
3. Catholic clergy active in politics, on behalf of their parties and social organisations.	3. Catholic clergy take no part in politics.

On the first two of these criteria, Malta is rather towards the open end of the spectrum. On the third, it is spectacularly near the closed end. In the introduction, I pointed out that there is no logical reason why a country should be at the same point in the spectrum on all three criteria: I claimed only that, in practice, one found that there was a rough correlation. The Maltese case shows that the correlation does not always apply. However, it is the only seriously anomalous instance that I have found. I did not feel obliged to abandon a pair of ideal types which fits most democracies quite well, on the ground that it fits one country badly.

The question may be asked – why does Malta deviate from the general pattern? The answer seems to be that the nature of the quarrel between the Church and politicians was different there from on the continent of Europe. On the continent, it had a settled philosophical basis: liberals and later socialists were ideologically opposed to the Church's values, and Catholics organised themselves in a sub-culture to counter them. In Malta, the two clashes which occurred were largely attributable to personalities; and though they were spectacular while they lasted, they were not of long duration. A parallel that occurs to an Irish observer is with the Parnell split of the eighteen-nineties. In 1890, the revelation of Parnell's adultery made many of his erstwhile followers feel that he was no longer suitable as leader of the Irish Parliamentary party, and a fierce quarrel ensued between those who remained loyal to him and those who rejected him. In this quarrel, the clergy came out violently against Parnell and were prominent in electioneering for his opponents. One would not therefore classify the Anti-Parnellites as a manifestation of closed Catholicism on the lines of the Christian Democratic parties of the continent. They were a movement of protest; they did not have as a basis the furtherance of Catholic social teaching. Moreover, the basis for the split was soon removed by Parnell's death, and a few years later the two parts of the Irish parliamentary party reunited. The picture of Ireland as a country where parties have not been organised on confessional principles remains unaffected.

Notes

Sources are cited as briefly as possible. They are given with just sufficient completeness to enable the full reference to be found in the bibliography.

Introduction (1–11)

1. The authorities were: Gary K. Bertsch *et al., Comparing Political Systems,* 20; Leon D. Epstein, *Political Parties in Western Democracies*, 3–4; T. T. Mackie and R. Rose, *The International Almanac of Electoral History*, ix; Douglas Rae, *The Political Consequences of Electoral Laws,* 7; R. Rose and D. W. Urwin, 'Persistence and change in party systems', 289. The countries securing one or two mentions were: Japan (2); Greece, Malta, Portugal, South Africa (1 each).
2. For Germany and the Netherlands, see R. Rose (ed.), *Electoral Behavior*, 148–9, 159–61, 249. For Switzerland, see Henry H. Kerr, *Switzerland: Social Cleavages and Partisan Conflict,* 11–13.
3. G. Michelat and M. Simon, *Classe, religion et comportement politique,* 310–12, 464, 463.

Chapter I (12–25)

1. For poll data see P. L. Reynolds, *The Democratic Labor Party*, 56–9; D. A. Kemp, *Society and Electoral Behaviour in Australia,* 194, 203.
2. H. F. Quinn, *The Union nationale*, 164–6.
3. The Irish hierarchy first appealed to the Irish party in this way in 1884: E. Larkin, *The Roman Catholic Church and the Creation of the Modern Irish State,* 244. The English bishops took longer, but in 1902 Cardinal Vaughan asked the Irish party to look after English Catholic educational interests: D. W. Miller, *Church, State and Nation in Ireland,* 79.
4. V. A. Lapomarda, 'A Jesuit runs for Congress', 209.
5. J. J. Kane, *Catholic-Protestant Conflicts in America*; Lerond Curry, *Protestant-Catholic Relations in America.*

6. G. Almond, 'Comparative political systems'; R. R. Alford, *Party and Society,* 50; R. Rose and D. W. Urwin, 'Persistence and change in party systems', R. Rose (ed.), *Electoral Behavior: A Comparative Handbook.* The last two authorities add a third category, the Scandinavian countries; however, the Scandinavian states are not considered in this book because their Catholic populations are negligible.
7. G. Almond, *art. cit.*
8. G. Sartori, 'European political parties: the case of polarized pluralism'; A. Lijphart, 'Typologies of democratic systems'.
9. S. M. Lipset and S. Rokkan, *Party Systems and Voter Alignments,* 1–64.

Chapter 2 (26–46)

1. J. and M. Hamelin, *Les moeurs électorales dans le Québec,* 35.
2. P. J. Jupp, 'Irish parliamentary elections and the influence of the Catholic vote', 187–90.
3. J. B. Artz, *France under the Bourbon Restoration,* 169.
4. See A. Simon, *Réunions des évêques de Belgique, 1830-1867,* 47, and the items by E. Witte in the bibliography. If my coverage were world-wide, I should at this point have had to mention Spain. In the Spanish elections of 1813–14, the clergy showed an activity which seems to have been unexampled elsewhere at that date. However, this precocity was not maintained. Throughout the rest of the nineteenth century, political change was achieved in Spain more often by force than by electioneering.
5. H. Metz, *Katholizismus und Wahlen,* 155.
6. For an excellent survey, see J. Gadille *et al., Les catholiques libéraux au XIXe siècle,* particularly the contribution by V. Conzemius, 'Les foyers internationaux du catholicisme libéral hors de France au XIXe siècle'.
7. *Enseignements pontificaux. L'éducation,* 5–23.
8. D. H. Fischer, *The Revolution of American Conservatism,* 223–5.
9. For American Catholic voting behaviour in the nineteenth century, see S. M. Lipset, 'Religion and politics in the American past and present', and A. M. Schlesinger (ed.), *History of U.S. Political Parties,* I, 514, 528, 530.
10. See C. H. Grattan, *The Southwest Pacific to 1900,* 141; J. G. Murtagh, *Australia: the Catholic Chapter,* 80, 88.
11. S. J. R. Noel, *Politics in Newfoundland,* 4–25.
12. P. G. Cornell, *The Alignment of Political Groups in Canada, 1841–1867,* 82, suggests that the French-Canadian majority was really a centre group which, when allied with Upper Canadian

reformers, had the aspect of a party of the 'left', and when allied with Upper Canadian conservatives after 1854 had the aspect of a party of the 'right'.

Chapter 3 (47–75)

1. J. Schauff, *Das Wahlverhalten der deutschen Katholiken*, 74, calculates the proportion of Catholics who voted for the Centre party in 1874 as 83 per cent. He makes careful allowances for (a) differential turnout, (b) differential levels of enfranchisement between Catholics and others (owing to a larger proportion of Catholics being under voting age), and (c) the voting patterns in Alsace-Lorraine and the Polish areas (where other parties attracted the Catholic vote). No figures are available from this period to indicate the proportion of Catholics who were practising, but it would hardly have been higher than 83 per cent. It seems safe to conclude, therefore, that in this election the Centre party mobilised just about all German-speaking practising Catholics.
2. E. Gruner, *Die Parteien in der Schweiz*, 30.
3. C. A. Macartney, *The Habsburg Empire,* 621, 683.
4. M. P. Fogarty, *Christian Democracy in Western Europe*, 208–9.
5. H. Jedin (ed.), *Handbuch der Kirchengeschichte,* VI/2, 505.
6. This analysis of Catholic schools of thought derives heavily from F. S. Nitti, *Catholic Socialism,* especially pp. 282–90.
7. B. Seebohm Rowntree, *Land and Labour: Lessons from Belgium,* 231–2.
8. It should be pointed out that Father Daens was suspended from his priestly functions because of his political activities. It is nevertheless symptomatic that this priest-politician should have emerged on the *left* of the official Catholic party.
9. L. Rosenbaum, *Beruf und Herkunft der Abgeordneten zu den deutschen und preussischen Parlamenten*, 23, 29.
10. D. P. Silverman, *Reluctant Union*, 114.
11. K. van Isacker, *Herderlijke brieven over politiek*, 7.
12. T. Nipperdey, *Die Organisation der deutschen Parteien*, 271n.
13. H. Dressel, *Die politischen Wahlen in der Stadt Trier*, 242.
14. W. Dittmar, *The Government of the Free State of Bavaria*, 139.
15. A. L. Lowell, *Governments and Parties in Continental Europe*, 339.
16. J. P. Charnay, *Les scrutins politiques en France*, tables 1–11 (no page numbers).
17. J. Gadille, *La pensée et l'action politiques des évêques français au début de la IIIe république,* II, 10, 68.
18. H. Daniel-Rops, *A Fight for God*, 104, 120.
19. E. Gruner, *Die Parteien in der Schweiz*, 79.

20. D. Blackbourn, 'The problem of democratisation: German Catholics and the role of the Centre party', 169.
21. C. H. D. Howard, 'The Parnell manifesto of 1885 and the schools question', 42–51.
22. J. H. Whyte, 'The influence of the Catholic clergy on elections in nineteenth-century Ireland', 252.
23. S. Mayor, *The Churches and the Labour Movement*, 114.
24. E. Larkin, 'Socialism and Catholicism in Ireland', 479.
25. Franz H. Mueller, 'The Church and the social question', 83.
26. J. Hulliger, *L'enseignement social des évêques canadiens*, 119.
27. *Ibid.*, 24–6.
28. P. Gleason, *The Conservative Reformers*, 61, 69ff, 85–6.
29. T. N. Brown, *Irish-American Nationalism*, 136, 142; S. T. McSeveney, *The Politics of Depression*, 138.
30. P. O'Farrell, *Harry Holland*, 92–4.
31. L. Lipson, *The Politics of Equality*, 224.
32. For information on Catholic voting behaviour in Britain see N. Blewett, *The Peers, the Parties and the People*, 350–3; P. F. Clarke, *Lancashire and the New Liberalism*, 253–9; H. Pelling, *Social Geography of British Elections*, especially pp. 16, 58, 233, 261, 353, 431; W. M. Walker, 'Irish immigrants in Scotland: their priests, politics and parochial life'; C. H. D. Howard, 'The Parnell manifesto of 1885 and the schools question'.
33. J. H. M. Laslett and S. M. Lipset (eds.), *Failure of a Dream? Essays in the History of American Socialism*, 238.
34. K. van Isacker, *Werkelijk en wettelijk land: de katholieke opinie tegenover de rechterzijde, 1863–84*. ['Pays réel' and 'pays légal': Catholic opinion with regard to the right wing in parliament, 1863–84].
35. U. Altermatt, *Der Weg der schweizer Katholiken ins Ghetto*. [The road of Swiss Catholics into the ghetto.]

Chapter 4 (76–99)

1. Calculated from the figures in D. Sternberger *et al.*, *Die Wahl der Parlamente*, 879, 1131. Most of my European election statistics come from this invaluable compilation.
2. S. H. Scholl, *150 jaar katholieke arbeidersbeweging in West-Europa*, 94.
3. M. Fogarty, *Christian Democracy in Western Europe*, 248.
4. A. Coutrot and F. Dreyfus, *Les forces religieuses dans la société française*, 55–6.
5. A. Latreille *et al.*, *Histoire du catholicisme en France*, III, 558–9.

6. Overall, the Dutch Nazi party received 7.94% of the vote. Provincial figures varied widely. The two most Catholic provinces provided both the best figure for the Nazis (Limburg: 11.69%) and the worst (N. Brabant: 2.93%). See G. A. Kooy, *Het echec van een 'volkse' beweging*, 285.
7. J. Beaufays, *Les partis catholiques en Belgique et aux Pay-Bas*, 573–4. The bishops threatened to refuse the sacraments to those who gave the party substantial support.
8. H. Müller, *Katholische Kirche und Nationalsozialismus*, 5–6, 13–23, 24–38.
9. For these terms see A. Diamant, *Austrian Catholics and the First Republic*, 16–22.
10. W. Bosworth, *Catholicism and Crisis in Modern France*, 254.
11. *Ibid.*, 241.
12. J. J. de Jong, *Overheid en Onderdaan*, 86, 97, 104, 113.
13. A. Coutrot and F. Dreyfus, *op. cit.*, 50.
14. W. Bosworth, *op. cit.*, 78.
15. Association française de science politique, *Les élections du 2 janvier 1956*, 132.
16. K. Steiner, *Politics in Austria*, 261–2; K. Shell, *The Transformation of Austrian Socialism*, 183–4.
17. J. Beaufays, *op. cit.*, 574–5.
18. H. Metz, *Katholizismus und Wahlen*, 133.
19. *Ibid.*, 135.
20. The Bishops of Liège and Bruges: J. Beaufays, *op. cit.*, 344, 742–4. Cardinal van Roey went almost as far: W. S. Plavsic, *Le Cardinal van Roey*, 184–5.
21. J. Beaufays, *op. cit.*, 577–81.
22. H. Metz, *op. cit.*, 172.
23. Quoted in G. Galli and A. Prandi, 'The Catholic hierarchy and Christian democracy in Italy', 355.
24. F. Spotts, *The Churches and Politics in Germany*, 315–18.
25. E. Gruner, *Die Parteien in der Schweiz*, 15, M. Fogarty, *Christian Democracy in Western Europe*, 247, states that this was founded as a ginger group within the larger Swiss farmers' interest group; but Gruner makes clear that it was intended as an interest group in its own right.
26. The movements referred to in this paragraph are treated at length in M. Fogarty, *op. cit.*, 232–93.
27. Percentages derived from figures in P. Waline, *Cinquante ans de rapports entre patrons et ouvriers en Allemagne*, II, 24, 96.
28. Murray G. Ballantyne, 'The Catholic Church and the C.C.F.', *Canadian Catholic Historical Association: Report 1963*, 34, 41.
29. C. T. Dienes, *Law, Politics and Birth Control*, 125, 131.

30. A. Abell, *American Catholicism and Social Action,* 262, states that the ACTU had fifteen chapters by 1940. *New Catholic Encyclopaedia,* I, 968, states that it had eleven chapters by 1941 and about the same fifteen years later.
31. R. R. Alford, *Party and Society,* 54.
32. R. S. Milne, *Political Parties in New Zealand,* 87.

Chapter 5 (100–16)

1. The complicated evolution of French Christian Democracy in recent years is skilfully unravelled by R. E. M. Irving, *The Christian Democratic Parties of Western Europe*, 222–31.
2. H. H. Kerr, 'Switzerland: Social Cleavages and Partisan Conflict', 16.
3. F. Spotts, *The Churches and German Politics,* 322.
4. K. Steiner, *Politics in Austria,* 338. The surveys on which this observation is based are dated 1965–6 in K. Liepelt, 'The infrastructure of party support in Germany and Austria', 183.
5. S. H. Barnes, *Representation in Italy,* 52, for 1968 data; H. Penniman (ed.), *Italy at the Polls,* 111, for 1975 data.
6. *Op. cit.,* 108.
7. *Op. cit.,* 51.
8. P. Waline, *Cinquante ans de rapports entre patrons et ouvriers en Allemagne,* II, 96.
9. K. Dobbelaere, J. Billiet and R. Creyf, 'Secularization and pillarization: a social problem approach', 120 note 14.
10. R. Metz and J. Schlick (eds.), *Politique et foi,* 46.
11. M. A. Fitzsimons (ed.), *The Catholic Church Today: Western Europe,* 260.
12. F. Huggett, *The Modern Netherlands,* 113.
13. H. Metz, *Katholizismus und Wahlen,* 71–2.
14. K. van Isacker, *Herderlijke brieven over politiek,* 170.
15. This development is outlined in Metz and Schlick, *op. cit.,* 74–9.
16. The process is explored in A. Langner (ed.), *Katholizismus und freiheitlicher Sozialismus in Europa.*
17. J. R. Frears, *Political Parties and Elections in the French Fifth Republic,* 119.
18. H. Penniman, *op. cit.,* 117.
19. R. Rémond, in Metz and Schlick, *op. cit.,* 84.
20. Quoted in P. Hebblethwaite, *The Runaway Church,* 160.
21. A. Coutrot and F. Dreyfus, *Les forces religieuses dans la société française,* 233.
22. J. A. van Kemenade, 'Roman Catholics and their schools', 22.
23. F. Spotts, *op. cit.,* 175.
24. Quoted in G. Picciotti, 'Il voto dei cattolici', 17.

25. P. M. Zulehner, *Wie kommen wir aus der Krise?*, 109.
26. Interdiocesaan centrum, Dienst voor godsdienststatistiek, *Basisstatistieken over de decanaten en bisdommen van de Belgische Kerkprovincie*, 81.
27. *Kirchliches Handbuch*, XXVI, 701; *ibid.*, XXVII, 149.
28. I have to thank Mr H. van Zoelen of the Katholiek Sociaal Kerkelijk Instituut in The Hague for providing me with these figures. They have since been published in M. M. J. van Hemert, *'En zij verontschuldigden zich . . . .'*, table 1.
29. J. Potel, 'Evolution récente de la pratique dominciale'.
30. *Op. cit.*, xxi.
31. For references see A. E. C. W. Spencer, 'Roman Catholic educational policy', in Philip Jebb (ed.), *Religious Education: Drift or Decision*, 166–8.
32. A. Greeley *et al.*, *Catholic Schools in a Declining Church*, 29.
33. Letter from Hugh Lindsay, Bishop of Hexham and Newcastle, *The Times*, 17 April 1975.
34. D. Martin, *A General Theory of Secularization*, 166 note 21.
35. The first pair of figures come from S. Crysdale and L. Wheatcroft (eds.), *Religion in Canadian Society*, 6; the second pair from the Canadian election studies of 1965 and 1974. I am much indebted to John H. Meisel and William P. Irvine of Queen's University, Kingston, for providing me with figures from the Canadian election studies. They show that the decline was even greater in Quebec (85% to 50%) than in the rest of Canada (68% to 47%).
36. J. H. Whyte, *Church and State in Modern Ireland 1923–1979*, 382.
37. H. Mol (ed.), *Western Religion*, 41.
38. A. Greeley *et al.*, *op. cit.*, 52, 57.
39. D. A. Kemp, *Society and Electoral Behaviour in Australia*, 196.
40. William P. Irvine, 'Explaining the religious basis of the Canadian partisan identity.'
41. A. Campbell *et al.*, *Elections and the Political Order*, 87–8, 96–112.
42. D. Knoke, 'Religion, stratification and politics: America in the 1960s', 344; R. Rose (ed.), *Electoral Behaviour*, 660. However, A. Greeley *et al.* (*op. cit.*, 76–102) emphasise how well the link between Catholicism and the Democratic party has held up, as do E. C. Ladd and C. P. Hadley, *Transformations of the American Party System*, 267–71. Norman H. Nie *et al.*, *The Changing American Voter*, 231, show that, if the proportion of Catholics identifying with the Democrats has dropped, the (much smaller) proportion of Catholics identifying with the Republicans has dropped even faster. The main movement has been into the group of those identifying with neither party.

43. C. T. Dienes, *Law, Politics and Birth Control,* 149–50, 201–7.
44. Edward Duff, S.J., in P. Gleason (ed.), *Contemporary Catholicism in the United States,* 118–19.
45. Mary T. Hanna, *Catholics and American Politics,* 37–44.
46. J. H. Whyte, *op. cit.,* 395–7.

Chapter 6 (117–29)

1. The interlocking effects of these two sets of factors have been well worked out for the United States by S. M. Lipset, 'Religion and politics in the American past and present'.
2. S. M. Lipset and S. Rokkan (eds.), *Party Systems and Voter Alignments,* 34.
3. H. Holborn, *A History of Modern Germany 1840–1945,* 356.

Appendix A. (130–4)

1. Another scholar who has shown an interest in constructing models of Catholic behaviour is Thomas C. Bruneau: see the titles in the bibliography under the heading 'general works'. His formulations are much less elaborate than Vallier's.
2. I. Vallier, in H. Landsberger (ed.), *The Church and Social Change in Latin America,* 19.

Appendix B. (135–44)

1. *Codex Iuris Canonici,* canons 859, 906, 1247–8.
2. F. Boulard and J. Rémy, *Pratique religieuse urbaine et régions culturelles,* 25n.
3. A notable source of data is the symposium edited by Hans Mol, *Western Religion.* This comprises articles on twenty-nine countries of Europe or of European settlement overseas. Most of the contributions contain information on religious practice. Unless otherwise stated, the figures given below derive from this book.
4. E. Bodzenta, *Die Katholiken in Österreich,* 74; P. M. Zulehner, *Wie kommen wir aus der Krise?,* 109, 118.
5. In H. Mol (ed.), *op. cit.,* 71.
6. R. Mols, 'La pratique dominicale en Belgique', 416.
7. F. Boulard and J. Rémy, *op. cit.,* 20.
8. *Ibid.,* 31.
9. *Kirchliches Handbuch,* XXVI, 701.
10. N. Greinacher, 'Auf dem Weg zur Gemeindekirche', in N. Greinacher and H. T. Risse (eds.), *Bilanz des deutschen Katholizismus,* 32. Dr Greinacher was head of the pastoral-sociological institute of the diocese of Essen.

11. S. Burgalassi, *Il comportamento religioso degli Italiani,* 26.
12. Katholiek sociaal-kerkelijk instituut, *Memo. 125,* 10.
13. J. J. Poeisz, 'The parishes of the Dutch Church province', 218.
14. J. J. de Jong, *Overheid en Onderdaan,* 182.
15. Cited in J. J. Poeisz, *op. cit.,* 218. I have not been able to obtain the original study.
16. H. Mol, *Religion in Australia,* 14.
17. S. Crysdale and L. Wheatcroft (eds.), *Religion in Canadian Society,* 6.
18. I am indebted to John F. Meisel and William P. Irvine for providing me with figures from this survey.
19. J. H. Whyte, *Church and State in Modern Ireland, 1923–1979,* 382.
20. S. Acquaviva, *The Decline of the Sacred in Industrial Society,* 63.
21. Cited in H. Mol, *Religion in Australia,* 16.
22. Figures provided by the (now defunct) Newman Demographic Survey, London.
23. R. Rose, *Governing without Consensus,* 496.
24. Cited in H. Mol, *Religion in Australia,* 16.
25. A. Greeley *et al., Catholic Schools in a Declining Church, 29.*
26. J. P. Alston, 'Social variables associated with church attendance', 234.

Appendix C. (145–8)

1. The General Workers' Union was founded in 1943. Among the principles accepted at its inaugural meeting was the maintenance of the best relations with the Church: E. Dobie, *Malta's Road to Independence,* 127.
2. E. Dobie, *op. cit.,* 93, 184, 210.
3. See the discussion above, pp. 88–91.
4. E. Dobie, *op. cit.,* 99.

Bibliography

This bibliography is arranged geographically. First are listed works with a general or world-wide coverage. Then come sections on continental Europe and on the Anglo-American world. Each of these is divided first into a sub-section on the region as a whole and then into subsections on individual countries, the countries being arranged alphabetically. Where a work has been useful for two or three countries, I have provided a full reference the first time the work is noted and a cross-heading under the other countries. Malta has a separate section at the end.

No attempt has been made at a complete coverage of the sources for the study of Catholic political behaviour, even for the thirteen countries examined in depth in this book. I have confined myself to citing those items which I personally found most useful, either because they provided precise information on a particular point, or because of their general treatment of a topic or period. Consequently, the bibliography contains three biases.

1. A linguistic bias: I have preferred to use sources in the languages I read more easily (English and French) rather than in those I read less easily (Dutch, German and Italian). I have therefore tended to consult works in the latter languages only when they were clearly better for a particular topic than those in English or French.
2. A bias in favour of items bearing directly on Catholic political behaviour: almost any general work on the history and politics of a particular country or group of countries will contain references to Catholicism, and I have consulted such works very extensively. I have not felt it necessary to cite them here, however, unless they had some substantial point to make about Catholic political activity.
3. A bias arising from the uneven distribution of the literature: some countries are much better served than others. Where the literature on a country is particularly rich, I have not attempted to cover it all, but have simply selected those items which seemed

most useful for my purposes. Specialists on France, Germany and Italy in particular will notice that there are many excellent works which I have not listed. On the other hand, for a country where there is no good book on Catholicism and politics, I have had to go quite deeply into periodical articles and general works on political history. This was particularly true of New Zealand, Britain and English-speaking Canada.

1. General works

Acquaviva, S. S., *The Decline of the Sacred in Industrial Society,* Oxford, 1979.

Aleixo, José Carlos, *The Catholic Church and Elections,* Cuernavaca, 1969, CIDOC: Sondeos, no. 62.

Almond, Gabriel A., 'Comparative political systems', *Journal of Politics* 18/2 (Aug. 1956), 391–409.

American Behavioral Scientist, 17/6 (July-August 1974). Special issue on 'The Church and modern society'.

Aubert, Roger, *Le pontificat de Pie IX,* Paris, 1952. A. Fliche et V. Martin (eds.), *Histoire de l'Église depuis les origines jusqu'à nos jours,* vol. 21.

Aubert, Roger, *et al.*, *The Church in a Secularised Society*, London, 1978. *The Christian Centuries,* vol. 5.

Bertsch, Gary K., Robert P. Clark and David M. Wood, *Comparing Political Systems: Power and Policy in Three Worlds,* New York, 1978.

Bihlmeyer, Karl, revised by Hermann Tüchle, *Church History, Vol. III: Modern and Recent Times,* Westminster, Md., 1966.

Bruneau, Thomas C., *The Political Transformation of the Brazilian Catholic Church,* Cambridge, England, 1974.*

Bruneau, Thomas C., 'Church and State in Portugal: crises of cross and sword' *A Journal of Church and State,* 18/3 (Autumn 1976), 463–90.*

Bruneau, Thomas C., 'Power and influence: analysis of the Church in Latin America and the case of Brazil', *Latin American Research Review,* 8 (1973), 25–51.*

Camp, Richard L., *The Papal Ideology of Social Reform,* Leiden, 1969.

Chenu, M.-D., *La "doctrine sociale" de l'Église comme idéologie,* Paris, 1979. (A study of the decline in a distinctive Catholic social teaching.)

Codex Iuris Canonici, Freiburg-im-Breisgau, 1918.

Dahl, Robert A. (ed.), *Political Oppositions in Western Democracies,* New Haven, 1965.

*These titles are included because of their relevance to the development of a general theory of Catholic political behaviour.

Daniel-Rops, H., *The Church in an Age of Revolution, 1789–1870,* London, 1965.

Daniel-Rops, H., *A Fight for God, 1870–1939,* London, 1966.

Enseignements pontificaux, Les. L'éducation: Présentation et tables par les moines de Solesmes, Tournai, 1956.

Epstein, Leon D., *Political Parties in Western Democracies,* London, 1967.

Falconi, Carlo, *The Popes in the Twentieth Century,* London, 1968.

Fitzsimons, M. A., and Waldemar Gurian (eds.), *The Catholic Church in World Affairs,* Notre Dame, 1954.

Gadille, Jacques, *et al., Les catholiques libéraux au XIXe siècle,* Grenoble, 1974.

Gestel, C. van, O. P., *La doctrine sociale de l'Église,* 3rd edn., Brussels, 1964.

Gnägi, Albert, *Katholische Kirche und Demokratie,* Zürich, 1970.

Gremillion, Joseph B., *The Catholic Movement of Employers and Managers,* Rome, 1961.

Hales, E. E. Y., *Pio Nono,* London, 1954.

Hales, E. E. Y., *Pope John and his Revolution,* London, 1966.

Hales, E. E. Y., *Revolution and Papacy, 1769–1846,* London, 1960.

Hastings, Adrian (ed.), *The Church and the Nations: a Study of Minority Catholicism,* London, 1959.

Hebblethwaite, Peter, *The Runaway Church,* 2nd edn., Glasgow, 1978. (A study of the Catholic Church since 1965.)

Hermet, Guy, 'Les fonctions politiques des organisations religieuses dans les régimes à pluralisme limité', *Revue française de science politique,* XXIII/3 (June 1973), 439–72.

International Labor Office, *Employers' and Workers' Participation in Planning,* Geneva, 1971.

Jebb, Dom Philip (ed.), *Religious Education: Drift or Decision?,* London, 1968.

Jedin, Hubert (ed.), *Handbuch der Kirchengeschichte, Band VI/1, Die Kirche zwischen Revolution und Restauration,* Freiburg-im-Breisgau, 1971.

Jedin, Hubert (ed.), *Handbuch der Kirchengeschichte, Band VI/2, Die Kirche zwischen Anpassung und Widerstand (1878 bis 1914),* Freiburg-im-Breisgau, 1973.

Jedin, Hubert, and Konrad Repgen (eds.), *Handbuch der Kirchengeschichte, Band VII, Die Weltkirche im 20. Jahrhundert,* Freiburg-im-Breisgau, 1979.

La Palombara, Joseph, and Myron Weiner (eds.), *Political Parties and National Development,* Princeton, 1966.

Latourette, Kenneth Scott, *Christianity in a Revolutionary Age: a History of Christianity in the Nineteenth and Twentieth Centuries,* London, 5 vols., 1959–63.

Leflon, Jean, *La crise révolutionnaire, 1789–1846,* Paris, 1948. A. Fliche et V. Martin (eds.), *Histoire de l'Église depuis les origines jusqu'à nos jours,* vol. 20.

Lewy, Guenther, *Religion and Revolution,* New York, 1974.

Lijphart, Arend, 'Religious vs. linguistic vs. class voting: the "crucial experiment" of comparing Belgium, Canada, South Africa, and Switzerland', *American Political Science Review*, 73/2 (June 1979), 442–58.

Lijphart, Arend, 'Typologies of democratic systems', *Comparative Political Studies*, I/1 (April 1968), 3–44.

Lipset, Seymour M., and Stein Rokkan (eds.), *Party Systems and Voter Alignments,* New York, 1967.

Mackie, Thomas T., and Richard Rose, *The International Almanac of Electoral History,* London, 1974.

McLaughlin, Sister M. Raymond, *Religious Education and the State,* Washington, 1967.

Martin, David, *A General Theory of Secularization,* Oxford, 1978.

Merle, Marcel (ed.), *Les églises chrétiennes et la décolonisation*, Paris, 1967.

Metz, René, and Jean Schlick (eds.), *Politique et foi: Troisième colloque du Cerdic, Strasbourg, 4–6 mai 1972*, Strasbourg, 1972.

Mol, Hans (ed.), *Western Religion,* The Hague, 1972.

Moody, Joseph N. (ed.), *Church and Society: Catholic Social and Political Thought and Movements, 1789–1950,* New York, 1953.

Moulin, Léo (ed.), *Les Eglises comme institutions politiques,* 2 vols., Brussels, 1973.

Mueller, Franz H., 'The Church and the social question', in Joseph N. Moody and Justus George Lawler (eds.), *The Challenge of Mater et Magistra,* New York, 1963, 13–154.

New Catholic Encyclopaedia, 15 vols., New York, 1967.

Newman, Jeremiah, *What is Catholic Action? An Introduction to the Lay Apostolate,* Westminster, Md., 1958.

Nichols, James Hastings, *Democracy and the Churches,* Philadelphia, 1951.

Nichols, Peter, *The Politics of the Vatican,* London, 1968.

Nitti, F. S., *Catholic Socialism,* London, 1895. (Translated from the second Italian edition.)

Noonan, John T., Jr., *Contraception,* Cambridge, Mass., 1966.

Noonan, John T., Jr. (ed.), *The Morality of Abortion: Legal and Historical Perspectives,* Cambridge, Mass., 1970.

Palmer, Robert R., *The Age of the Democratic Revolution: a Political History of Europe and America, 1760–1800,* 2 vols., Princeton, 1959–64.

Poulat, Émile, *Église contre bourgeoisie: Introduction au devenir du catholicisme actuel,* Paris, 1977.

Rae, Douglas, *The Political Consequences of Electoral Laws,* 2nd edn., New Haven, 1971.

Rogier, L. J., G. de Bertier de Sauvigny and Joseph Hajjar, *Siècle des lumières, révolutions, restaurations,* Paris, 1966. *Nouvelle histoire de l'Église,* vol. 4.

Rose, Richard (ed.), *Electoral Behaviour: a Comparative Handbook,* New York, 1974.

Rose, Richard, and Derek W. Urwin, 'Social cohesion, political parties and strains in regimes', *Comparative Political Studies,* 2 (1969), 7–67.

Rose, Richard, and Derek W. Urwin, 'Persistence and change in western party systems since 1945', *Political Studies,* 18/3 (Sept. 1970), 287–319.

Sánchez, José, *Anticlericalism: a Brief History,* Notre Dame, 1972.

Sartori, Giovanni, 'European Political parties: the case of polarized pluralism', in Joseph La Palombara and Myron Weiner (eds.), *Political Parties and National Development,* Princeton, 1966, 137–76.

Silvert, Kalman H. (ed.), *Churches and States: the Religious Institution and Modernization,* New York, 1967.

Sturmthal, Adolf, *Comparative Labor Movements: Ideological Roots and Institutional Development,* Belmont, Cal., 1972.

Sturzo, Luigi, *Church and State,* Notre Dame, 1962.

Vallier, Ivan, *Catholicism, Social Control, and Modernization in Latin America,* Englewood Cliffs, 1970.*

Vallier, Ivan, 'Extraction, insulation, and re-entry: toward a theory of religious change', in Henry A. Landsberger (ed.), *The Church and Social Change in Latin America,* Notre Dame, 1970, 9–35.*

Westhues, Kenneth, 'The Church in opposition', *Sociological Analysis,* 37/4 (1976), 283–97.

2. Continental Europe

A. General Works

Some of the works under this heading refer also to Britain and Ireland.

Alix, Christine, *Le Saint-Siège et les nationalismes en Europe, 1870–1960,* Paris, 1962.

Almond, Gabriel, 'The Christian parties of western Europe', *World Politics,* I/1 (Oct. 1948), 30–58.

*These titles are included because of their relevance to the development of a general theory of Catholic political behaviour.

Almond, Gabriel A., 'The resistance and the political parties of western Europe', *Political Science Quarterly,* 62/1 (Mar. 1947), 27–61.

Anderson, Eugene N., and Pauline R. Anderson, *Political Institutions and Social Change in Continental Europe in the Nineteenth Century,* Berkeley and Los Angeles, 1967.

Binkley, Robert C., *Realism and Nationalism,* 1852–1871, New York, 1935.

Boulard, Fernand, and Jean Rémy, *Pratique religieuse urbaine et régions culturelles,* Paris, 1968.

Bouscaren, Anthony T., 'The European Christian Democrats', *Western Political Quarterly,* II/1 (Mar. 1949), 59–73.

Chadwick, Owen, *The Secularization of the European Mind in the Nineteenth Century,* Cambridge, England, 1975.

Fitzsimons, M. A. (ed.), *The Catholic Church Today: Western Europe,* Notre Dame, 1969.

Fogarty, Michael P., *Christian Democracy in Western Europe, 1820–1953,* London, 1957.

Galenson, Walter, *Trade Union Democracy in Western Europe,* Berkeley: Los Angeles, 1961.

Hayes, Carlton J. H., *A Generation of Materialism, 1871–1900,* New York, 1941.

Helmreich, Ernst C. (ed.), *A Free Church in a Free State?,* Boston, 1964.

Henig, Stanley (ed.), *Political Parties in the European Community,* London, 1979.

Henig, Stanley, and John Pinder (eds.), *European Political Parties,* London, 1969.

Irving, R. E. M., *The Christian Democratic Parties of Western Europe,* London, 1979.

Irving, R. E. M., 'Christian Democracy in post-war Europe: conservatism writ-large or distinctive political phenomenon?', *West European Politics,* 2/1 (Jan. 1979), 53–68.

Jong, J. J. de, *Overheid en onderdaan,* Wageningen, 1956. (The first comparative study of voting behaviour across European democracies.)

Kothen, Robert, *La pensée et l'action sociales des Catholiques, 1789–1944,* Louvain, 1945.

Landauer, Carl, *European Socialism: a History of Ideas and Movements from the Industrial Revolution to Hitler's Seizure of Power,* 2 vols., Berkeley: Los Angeles, 1959.

Langner, Albrecht (ed.), *Katholizismus und freiheitlicher Sozialismus in Europa,* Cologne, 1965.

Lijphart, Arend, *Class Voting and Religious Voting in the European*

Democracies, Glasgow: University of Strathclyde Survey Research Centre, Occasional Paper no. 8, 1971.

Lowell, A. Lawrence, *Governments and Parties in Continental Europe,* 2 vols., Cambridge, Mass., 1896.

Maier, Hans, *Revolution and Church: the Early History of Christian Democracy, 1789–1901,* Notre Dame, 1969. (First published in German, 1965).

Ogg, F. A., *The Governments of Europe,* New York, 1913.

Rhodes, Anthony, *The Vatican in the Age of the Dictators 1922–1945,* London, 1973.

Scholl, S. H. (ed.), *150 ans de mouvement ouvrier chrêtien,* Louvain, 1966.

Smith, Gordon, *Politics in Western Europe,* London, 1972.

Sternberger, Dolf, Bernhard Vogel and Dieter Nohlen, *Die Wahl der Parlamente und anderer Staatsorgane: ein Handbuch, Band I: Europa,* 2 vols., Berlin, 1969.

Vidler, Alec R., *A Century of Social Catholicism, 1820–1920,* 2nd edn., London, 1969.

Wallace, Lilian Parker, *Leo XIII and the Rise of Socialism,* Durham, N.C., 1966.

Wallace, Lilian Parker, *The Papacy and European Diplomacy, 1869–1878,* Chapel Hill, 1948.

Wilson, Stephen, 'Nationalism, Catholicism and the Church in Europe', *Clergy Review,* LXI/12 (Dec. 1976), 477–86.

B. Austria

Barker, Elisabeth, *Austria, 1918–1972,* London, 1973.

Bluhm, William T., *Building an Austrian Nation: the Political Integration of a Western State,* New Haven, 1973.

Bodzenta, Erich, *Die Katholiken in Österreich: ein religionssoziologischer Überblick,* Vienna, 1962.

Boyer, John W., 'Catholic priests in Lower Austria: anti-liberalism, occupational anxiety, and radical political action in late nineteenth-century Vienna', *Proceedings of the American Philosophical Society,* 118/4 (Aug. 1974), 337–69.

Diamant, Alfred, *Austrian Catholics and the First Republic,* Princeton, 1960.

Freund, Fritz, *Das österreichische Abgeordnetenhaus: ein biographisch-statistisches Handbuch,* Vienna, 1907.

Jenks, William Alexander, *The Austrian Electoral Reform of 1907,* New York, 1950.

Klemperer, Klemens von, *Ignaz Seipel: Christian Statesman in a Time of Crisis,* Princeton, 1962.

Knoll, Reinhold, *Zur Tradition der christlichsozialen Partei: ihre Früh- und Entwicklungsgeschichte bis zu der Reichsratwahlen 1907,* Vienna, 1973.

Lewis, Gavin, 'The peasantry, rural change and conservative agrarianism: Lower Austria at the turn of the century', *Past and Present,* 81 (Nov. 1978), 119–43.

Liepelt, Klaus, 'The infra-structure of party support in Germany and Austria', in Mattei Dogan and Richard Rose (eds.), *European Politics, a Reader,* Boston, 1971, 183–202.

Macartney, C. A., *The Habsburg Empire, 1790–1918,* London, 1968.

Shell, Kurt, *The Transformation of Austrian Socialism,* New York, 1962.

Simons, Thomas W., Jr., 'Vienna's first Catholic political movement: the Güntherians, 1848–1857', *Catholic Historical Review,* LV/2 (July 1969), 173–94; 3 (Oct. 1969), 377–93; 4 (Jan. 1970), 610–26.

Steiner, Kurt, *Politics in Austria,* Boston, 1972.

Stiefbold, Rodney, Arlette Leupold-Löwenthal, Georg Ress, Walther Lichem and Dwaine Marvick, *Wahlen und Parteien in Österreich,* 3 vols., Vienna, 1966.

Zulehner, Paul Michael, *Wie kommen wir aus der Krise? Kirchliche Statistik Österreichs 1945–1975 und ihre pastoralen Konsequenzen,* Vienna, 1978.

C. Belgium

Aubert, Roger, 'Le cardinal van Roey', *Revue nouvelle,* XXXIV/8–9 (Aug–Sept. 1961), 113–30.

Aubert, Roger, 'L'Eglise catholique et la vie politique en Belgique depuis la seconde guerre mondiale', *Res Publica, XV/2 (1973),* 183–203.

Aubert, Roger, 'L'Eglise et L'Etat en Belgique au XIXe siècle', *Res Publica,* X (1968), 9–31 (Special number on 'les problèmes constitutionnels de la Belgique au XIXe siècle'.)

Bartier, J., 'Partis politiques et classes sociales en Belgique', *ibid.,* 33–106.

Beaufays, Jean, *Les partis catholiques en Belgique et aux Pays-Bas 1918–1958,* Brussels, 1973.

Billiet, Jaak, 'Secularization and compartmentalization in the Belgian educational system: an analysis of the problems relevant to the revision of the school pact', *Social Compass,* XX (1973/4), 569–91.

Billiet, J., and K. Dobbelaere, *Godsdienst in Vlaanderen: van kerks katolicisme naar sociaal-kulturele kristenheid,* Leuven, 1976.

Dobbelaere, K., J. Billiet and R. Creyf, 'Secularization and pillarization: a social problem approach', *Annual Review of the Social Sciences of Religion,* 2 (1978), 97–124.

Etienne, Jean-Michel, *Le mouvement rexiste jusqu'en 1940,* Paris, 1968.

Frognier, André-Paul, 'Vote, classe sociale et religion/pratique religieuse', *Res Publica,* 17/4 (1975), 479–90.

Interdiocesaan centrum. Dienst voor godsdienststatistiek, *Basis-statistieken over de decanaten en bisdommen van de Belgische Kerk-provincie,* Brussels, n.d. (1973?).

Isacker, Karel van, S. J., *Het Daensisme,* Antwerp, 1959.

Isacker, Karel van, S.J., *Herderlijke brieven over politiek 1830/1966,* Antwerp, 1969.

Isacker, Karel van, S.J., *Werkelijk en wettelijk land: de katholieke opinie tegenover de rechterzijde 1863–1884,* Antwerp, 1955.

Kossmann, E. H., *The Low Countries 1780–1940,* Oxford, 1978.

Lorwin, Val R., 'Labour unions and political parties in Belgium', *Industrial and Labour Relations Review,* 28/2 (Jan. 1975), 243–63.

Luykx, Theo, *Politieke geschiedenis van België, van 1789 tot heden,* 4th edn., 2 vols., Brussels, 1979.

Mallinson, Vernon, *Power and Politics in Belgian Education, 1815 to 1961,* London, 1963.

Mols, Roger, S.J., 'La pratique dominicale en Belgique: situation actuelle et évolution récente', *Nouvelle revue théologique,* 93/4 (April 1971), 387–424.

Plavsic, Wladimir S., *Le cardinal van Roey,* Brussels, 1974.

Plavsic, Wladimir S., 'L'Eglise et la politique en Belgique', *Res Publica,* X/2 (1968), 211–51.

Revue nouvelle, LVI/9 (Sept. 1972): symposium on 'Vers l'école pluraliste?' 113–58.

Rowntree, B. Seebohm, *Land and Labour: Lessons from Belgium,* London, 1910.

Simon, A., *Catholicisme et politique: documents inédits (1832–1909),* Wetteren, 1955.

Simon, A., *L'Eglise catholique et les débuts de la Belgique indépendante,* Wetteren, 1949.

Simon, A., 'L'influence de l'Eglise sur la vie politique dans l'entre deux guerres', *Res Publica,* IV (1962), 387–401.

Simon, A., *Le parti catholique belge, 1830–1945,* Brussels, 1958.

Simon, A., *Réunions des évêques de Belgique, 1830–867: procès verbaux,* Louvain, 1960.

Seiler, Daniel, *Le déclin du cléricalisme,* Brussels, 1975.

Vaussard, Maurice, *Histoire de la démocratie chrétienne: France – Belgique – Italie,* Paris, 1956.

Verkade, W., *Democratic Parties in the Low Countries and Germany,* Leiden, 1965.

Voyé, Liliane, *Sociologie du geste religieux: de l'analyse de la pratique dominicale en Belgique à une interprétation théorique,* Brussels, 1973.

Witte, Els, 'Electorale agenten aan de vooravond van de partijformaties', *Revue belge d'histoire contemporaine*, I/2 (1969), 216–53.

Witte, Els, 'Les évêques belges et les élections de 1830 à 1847: état de la question', in *L'Eglise et l'Etat à l'époque contemporaine. Mélanges dédiés à la mémoire de mgr Alois Simon*, Brussels, 1975.

Witte, Els, *Politieke machtsstrijd in en om de voornaamste Belgische steden, 1830–1848*, 2 vols., Brussels, 1973.

D. France

Adam, Gérard, 'De la C.F.T.C. à la C.F.D.T.', *Revue française de science politique*', XV/1 (Feb. 1965), 87–103.

Anderson, Malcolm, *Conservative Politics in France*, London, 1974.

Artz, Frederick B., *France under the Bourbon Restoration, 1814-1830*, Cambridge, Mass., 1931.

Assemblée plénière de l'épiscopat français, *Pour une pratique chrétienne de la politique*, Paris, 1972. (Joint pastoral letter.)

Association française de science politique, *Les élections du 2 janvier 1956*, Paris, 1957.

Berger, Suzanne, *Peasants against Politics: Rural Organization in Brittany, 1911–1967*, Cambridge, Mass., 1972.

Bosworth, William, *Catholicism and Crisis in Modern France*, Princeton, 1962.

Boulard, Fernand, *Premiers itinéraires en sociologie religieuse*, Paris, 1955.

Charnay, Jean-Paul, 'L'Eglise catholique et les élections françaises', *Politique*, 19–20 (Jul.–Dec. 1962), 257–306.

Charnay, Jean-Paul, *Les scrutins politiques en France de 1815 à 1962*, Paris, 1964.

Charnay, Jean-Paul, *Le suffrage politique en France*, Paris: The Hague, 1965.

Cobban, Alfred, 'The influence of the clergy and the instituteurs primaires in the election of the French constituent assembly, April 1948', in A. Cobban, *France since the Revolution, and other aspects of modern history*, London, 1970.

Coutrot, Aline, and François G. Dreyfus, *Les forces religieuses dans la société française*, Paris, 1965.

Dansette, Adrian, *A Religious History of Modern France*, 2 vols., Edinburgh, 1961.

Domenach, Jean-Marie, and Robert de Montvalon, *The Catholic Avant-Garde: French Catholicism since World War II*, New York, 1967.

Duroselle, J. B., 'L'attitude politique et sociale des catholiques français en 1848', *Revue d'Histoire de l'Église de France*, XXXIV (1948), 44–62.

Duverger, Maurice (ed.), *Partis politiques et classes sociales en France*,

Paris, 1955.
Einaudi, Mario, and Goguel, François, *Christian Democracy in Italy and France*, Notre Dame, 1952.
Elbow, Matthew H., *French Corporative Theory, 1789–1948*, New York, 1953.
Frears, J. R., *Political Parties and Elections in the French Fifth Republic*, London, 1977.
Gadille, Jacques, *La pensée et l'action politiques des évêques français au début de la IIIe république, 1870–1883*, 2 vols., Paris, 1967.
Goguel, François, *La politique des partis sous la IIIe république*, 3rd edn., Paris, 1958.
Goguel, François (ed.), *Le référendum d'octobre et les élections de novembre 1962*, Paris, 1965.
Gouley, Bernard, *Les catholiques français aujourd'hui*, Paris, 1977.
Hainsworth, Paul, 'Towards a new ralliement? Left-wing unity and the Catholic policy of the French Communist Party', *Parliamentary Affairs*, XXX/4 (Autumn 1977), 427–42.
Irving, R. E. M., *Christian Democracy in France*, London, 1973.
Latreille, A., J.-R. Palanque, E. Delaruelle and R. Rémond, *Histoire du Catholicisme en France, III: La période contemporaine*, Paris, 1962.
McManners, John, *Church and State in France, 1870–1914*, London, 1972.
Mayeur, J.-M., *et al.*, *L'histoire religieuse de la France, 19e–20e siècle: problèmes et méthodes*, Paris, 1975.
Michelat, Guy, and Michel Simon, *Classe, religion et comportement politique*, Paris, 1977.
Michelat, Guy, and Michel Simon, 'Religion, class and politics', *Comparative Politics*, 10/1 (Oct. 1977), 159–86.
Potel, Julien, 'Evolution récente de la pratique dominicale', *La Maison-Dieu*, 130 (1977), 35–48.
Prélot, Marcel, 'Histoire et doctrine du parti démocrate populaire', *Politique*, 19–20 (Jul.–Dec. 1962), 307–40.
Rémond, René, 'Droite et gauche dans le catholicisme français contemporain', *Revue française de science politique*, VIII/3, (Sept. 1958), 529–44, and 4 (Dec. 1958), 803–20.
Rémond, René, *The Right Wing in France from 1815 to de Gaulle*, Philadelphia, 1966.
Reynard, Jean-Daniel, 'Trade unions and political parties in France: some recent trends', *Industrial and Labor Relations Review*, 28/2 (Jan. 1975), 208–25.
Silverman, Dan P., *Reluctant Union: Alsace-Lorraine and Imperial Germany, 1871 -1918*, University Park, Pa., 1972.
Vaussard, Maurice – see under Belgium.
Vidler, Alec R., *Prophecy and Papacy: a study of Lamennais, the Church*

and the Revolution, London, 1954.

Williams, Philip, *Crisis and Compromise: Politics in the Fourth Republic*, London, 1964.

E. Germany

Amery, Carl, *Capitulation: the Lesson of German Catholicism*, New York, 1967.

Blackbourn, David G., 'The problem of democratisation: German Catholics and the role of the Centre party', in Richard J. Evans (ed.), *Society and Politics in Wilhelmine Germany*, London, 1978.

Buchheim, Karl, *Geschichte der christlichen Parteien in Deutschland*, Munich, 1953.

Burnham, Walter Dean, 'Political immunization and political confessionalism: the United States and Weimar Germany', *Journal of Interdisciplinary History*, III/1 (Summer 1972), 1–30.

Dittmar, W. R., *The Government of the Free State of Bavaria*, Williamsport, Pa., 1934.

Dowell, J. D., 'Uneasy allies: Catholics and Christian Democrats in West Germany', *Australian Journal of Politics and History*, XVIII/3 (Dec. 1972), 360–6.

Dressel, Hilmar, *Die politischen Wahlen in der Stadt Trier und in den Eifel- und Moselkreisen des Regierungsbezirks Trier 1888–1913*, Bonn: doctoral dissertation, 1962.

Dru, Alexander, *The Church in the Nineteenth Century: Germany 1800–1918*, London, 1963.

Greinacher, Norbert, and H. T. Risse (eds.), *Bilanz des deutschen Katholizismus*, Mainz, 1966.

Hartweg, Frédéric, 'Les églises, les partis et les élections de 1976', *Revue d'Allemagne*, 9/2 (April–June 1977), 231–54.

Helmreich, Ernst Christian, *Religious Education in German Schools*, Cambridge, Mass., 1959.

Holborn, Hajo, *A History of Modern Germany 1840–1945*, New York, 1969.

Irving, R. E. M., and W. E. Paterson, 'The West German parliamentary election of November 1972', *Parliamentary Affairs*, 26/2 (1972–3), 218–39.

Kaase, Max, and Klaus von Beyme (eds.), *Elections and Parties*, London, 1978. *German Political Studies*, vol. 3.

Kirchliches Handbuch: ämtliches statistisches Jahrbuch der katholischen Kirche Deutschlands, Band XXVI: 1962–1968, Cologne, 1969; *Band XXVII: 1969–1974*, Cologne, 1975.

Kitzinger, U. W., *German Electoral Politics: a Study of the 1957 Campaign*, Oxford, 1960.

Liepelt, Klaus – see under Austria.

Metz, Hubert, *Katholizismus und Wahlen: zum Verhältnis Kirche und Staat in Deutschland*, Mannheim: doctoral dissertation, 1976.

Milatz, Alfred, *Wähler und Wahlen in der Weimarer Republik*, Bonn, 1965.

Morsey, Rudolf, *Der Untergang des politischen Katholizismus: die Zentrumspartei zwischen christlichem Selbstverständnis und 'Nationaler Erhebung' 1923/33*, Stuttgart, 1977.

Müller, Hans, *Katholische Kirche und Nationalsozialismus: Dokumente 1930–1935*, Munich, 1963.

Nipperdey, Thomas, *Die Organisation der deutschen Parteien vor 1918*, Düsseldorf, 1961.

Noakes, Jeremy, and Geoffrey Pridham (eds.), *Documents on Nazism, 1919–1945*, London, 1974.

Pridham, Geoffrey, *Hitler's Rise to Power: the Nazi Movement in Bavaria, 1923–1933*, London, 1973.

Rauscher, Anton (ed.), *Kirche – Politik – Parteien*, Cologne, 1974.

Rosenbaum, L., *Beruf und Herkunft der Abgeordneten zu den deutschen und preussischen parliamenten, 1847 bis 1919*, Frankfurt-am-Main, 1923.

Ross, Ronald J., *Beleaguered Tower: the Dilemma of Political Catholicism in Wilhelmine Germany*, Notre Dame, 1976.

Roth, Guenther, *The Social Democrats in Imperial Germany*, Totowa, N.J., 1963.

Rovan, Joseph, *Le catholicisme politique en Allemagne*, Paris, 1956.

Steil, Hans Willi, *Die politischen Wahlen in der Stadt Trier und in den Eifel- und Moselkreisen des Regierungsbezirks Trier 1867–1887*, Bonn: doctoral dissertation, 1961.

Schauff, Johannes, ed. by Rudolf Morsey, *Das Wahlverhalten der deutschen Katholiken im Kaiserreich und in der Weimarer Republik: Untersuchungen aus dem Jahre 1928*, Mainz, 1975.

Schmidtchen, Gerhard, *Protestanten und Katholiken*, Bern and Munich, 1973.

Silverman, Dan P. – see under France.

Spotts, Frederick, *The Churches and Politics in Germany*, Middletown, Conn., 1973.

Tallen, Hermann, *Die Auseinandersetzung über § 218 StGB: zu einem Konflikt zwischen der SPD und der Katholischen Kirche*, Munich, 1977. (On the abortion controversy of 1970–6.)

Tinnemann, Sister Ethel Mary, S.N.J.M., 'Attitudes of the German Catholic Hierarchy toward the Nazi regime: a study in German psycho-political culture', *Western Political Quarterly*, XXII/2 (June 1969), 333–49.

Trzeciakowski, Lech, 'The Prussian State and the Catholic Church in Prussian Poland 1871–1914', *Slavic Review*, XXVI/4 (Dec. 1967), 618–37.

Verkade, Willem – see under Belgium.

Waline, Pierre, *Cinquante ans de rapports entre patrons et ouvriers en Allemagne, Tome II: depuis 1945,* Paris, 1970.

Willey, Richard J., 'Trade unions and political parties in the Federal Republic of Germany', *Industrial and Labour Relations Review,* 28/1 (Oct. 1974), 35–59.

Windell, George G., *The Catholics and German Unity, 1866–1871,* Minneapolis, 1954.

Zangerl, Carl H. E., 'Courting the Catholic vote: the Center party in Baden, 1903–13', *Central European History,* X/3 (Sept. 1977), 220–40.

Zeender, John K., 'German Catholics and the concept of an interconfessional party, 1900–1922', *Journal of Central European Affairs,* XXIII (1964), 424–39.

Zeender, John K., *The German Center Party 1890–1906,* Philadelphia, 1976.

F. Italy

Allum, Peter, *Italy – Republic without Government?,* London, 1973.

Barnes, Samuel H., *Representation in Italy: Institutionalized Tradition and Electoral Choice,* Chicago, 1977.

Buonaiuti, Cesare Marongiu, *Non expedit: storia di una politica (1866–1919),* Milan, 1971.

Binchy, D. A., *Church and State in Fascist Italy,* London, 1941.

Burgalassi, Silvano, *Il comportamento religioso degli Italiani,* Florence, 1968.

Chassériaud, J. P., *Le parti démocrate chrétien en Italie,* Paris, 1965.

Einaudi, M., and F. Goguel – see under France.

Galli, Giorgio, and Alfonso Prandi, 'The Catholic hierarchy and Christian Democracy in Italy', in Mattei Dogan and Richard Rose (eds.), *European Politics: a Reader,* London, 1971.

Godechot, Thierry, *Le parti démocrate-chrétien italien,* Paris, 1964.

Irving, R. E. M., and Martin Clark, 'The Italian political crisis and the general election of May 1972', *Parliamentary Affairs,* 25/3 (1972), 198–223.

Jemolo, A. C., *Church and State in Italy,* Oxford, 1960.

LaPalombara, Joseph, *Interest Groups in Italian Politics,* Princeton, 1964.

Picciotti, Giulio, 'Il voto dei cattolici', *Nord e sud,* 17/126 (June 1970), 13–32.

Prandi, Alfonso, *Chiesa e politica: la Gerarchia e l'impegno politico dei cattolici italiani,* Bologna, 1968.

Seton-Watson, Christopher, *Italy from Liberalism to Fascism, 1870–1925,* London, 1967.

Settembrini, Domenico, *La Chiesa nella politica italiana 1944–1963,* Pisa, 1964.

Social Compass, XXIII/2–3 (1976). (Special number on 'Politics and religion in Italy'.)

Vaussard, Maurice – see under Belgium.

Webster, Richard A., *The Cross and the Fasces: Christian Democracy and Fascism in Italy,* Stanford, 1960.

Zariski, Raphael, *Italy: the Politics of Uneven Development*, Hinsdale, Ill., 1972.

G. The Netherlands

Beaufays, J. – see under Belgium.

Bisschoppelijk mandement, *De katholiek in het openbare leven van deze tijd*, Zeist, 1954.

Bornewasser, J. A., 'Mythical aspects of Dutch anti-Catholicism in the nineteenth century', in J. S. Bromley and E. H. Kossman (eds.), *Britain and the Netherlands, vol. V: Some Political Mythologies,* The Hague, 1975.

Brachin, Pierre, and L. J. Rogier, *Histoire du catholicisme hollandais depuis le XVIe siècle,* Paris, 1974.

Coleman, John A., *The Evolution of Dutch Catholicism 1958–1974,* Berkeley: Los Angeles, 1978.

Gribling, J. P., 'Uit de geschiedenis van de R.K.S.P.', *Politiek Perspectief,* 5/6 (1976), 1–71.

Heijden, M. J. M. van der, *De dageraad van de emancipatie der katholieken: de nederlandsche katholieken en de staatkundige verwikkelingen uit het laatste kwart van de achttiende eeuw,* Nijmegen, 1947.

Hemert, M. M. J. van, *'En zij verontschuldigden zich .....' de ontwikkeling van het misbezoek cijfer 1966–1979,* The Hague, 1980. KASKI memorandum no. 213.

Huggett, Frank E., *The Modern Netherlands,* London, 1971.

Katholiek sociaal-kerkelijk instituut, *Memo. 125: De katholieke bevolking van Nederland naar enkele gezichtspunten van de gegevens der kerkelijke registratie en statistiek per 1-1-1960,* The Hague, 1961.

Kemenade, J. A. van, 'Roman Catholics and their schools', *Sociologia Neerlandica,* 7/1 (1971), 15–27.

Kooy, G. A., *Het echec van een 'volkse' beweging: Nazificatie en denazificatie in Nederland 1931–1945,* Assen, 1964.

Kossmann, E. H. – see under Belgium.

Lijphart, Arend, *The Politics of Accommodation: Pluralism and Democracy in the Netherlands,* 2nd edn., Berkeley: Los Angeles, 1975.

Lipschits, I., *Politieke stromingen in Nederland: inleiding tot de geschiedenis van de Nederlandse politieke partijen,* Deventer, 1977.

De Nederlandse kiezer '72, Alphen aan den Rijn, 1973.
De Nederlandse kiezer '77, Voorschoten, 1977.
Plas, Michel van der, *Uit het rijke Roomsche leven: een documentaire over de jaren 1925–1935,* Utrecht, 1964.
Poeisz, Jos. J., 'The parishes of the Dutch Church Province, 1-1-1966', *Social Compass,* XIV/3 (1967), 203–31.
Roes, Jan, 'R. K. Kerk Nederland, 1958–1973: een encyclopedisch overzicht', *Archief voor de geschiedenis van de Katholieke Kerk in Nederland,* 16/1 (1974), 73–141.
Rogier, L. J., *Katholieke herleving: geschiedenis van katholiek Nederland sinds 1853,* The Hague, 1956.
Scholten, L. W. G., *et al., De confessionelen,* Utrecht, 1968.
Steeman, Th.M., 'L'Eglise d'aujourd'hui: une exploration de la Hollande Catholique en 1966', *Social Compass,* XIV/3 (1967), 165–202.
Thurlings, J. M. G., 'The case of Dutch Catholicism: a contribution to the theory of the pluralistic society', *Sociologia Neerlandica,* 7 (1971), 118–36.
Thurlings, J. M. G., *De wankele zuil: Nederlandse katholieken tussen assimilatie en pluralisme,* 2nd edn., Deventer, 1978.
Vellenga, S. Y. A., *Katholiek Zuid Limburg en het fascisme,* Assen, 1975.
Verkade, W. – see under Belgium.
Witlox, J. H. J. M., *De staatkundige emancipatie van Nederlandse katholieken 1848–1870,* Bussum, 1969.
Windmuller, John P., *Labor Relations in the Netherlands,* Ithaca, N.Y., 1969.

H. Switzerland

Altermatt, Urs, *Der Weg der Schweizer Katholiken ins Ghetto,* Zürich, 1972.
Altermatt, Urs, and Hans Peter Fagagnini (eds.), *Die CVP zwischen Programm und Wirklichkeit,* Zürich, 1979.
Boltanski, Luc, *Le bonheur suisse,* Paris, 1966.
Bonjour, E., H. S. Offler and G. R. Potter, *A Short History of Switzerland,* Oxford, 1952.
Conrad, Carl-August, *Die politischen Parteien im Verfassungssystem der Schweiz,* 1970.
Fischer, E., *Histoire de la Suisse,* Paris, 1946.
Girod, R., 'Clivages confessionnels et gouvernement de tous les partis', *Revue suisse de sociologie,* 3/3 (Nov. 1977), 93–104.
Gruner, Erich, *Die Parteien in der Schweiz,* Berne, 1969.
Gruner, Erich (ed.), *Die Schweiz seit 1945,* Berne, 1971.
Handbuch der Schweizer Geschichte, Band 2, Zürich, 1977.
Kerr, Henry H., Jr., *Switzerland: Social Cleavages and Partisan Conflict,*

London: Beverley Hills, 1972. Sage Contemporary Political Sociology Series, no. 06–002.

Rappard, William, *La constitution fédérale de la Suisse, 1848–1948,* Boudry: Neuchâtel, 1948.

Ruffieux, Roland, *La Suisse de l'entre-deux-guerres,* Lausanne, 1974.

Siegenthaler, Jürg K., 'Current problems of trade union-party relations in Switzerland: reorientation versus inertia', *Industrial and Labour Relations Review,* 28/2 (Jan. 1975), 264–81.

Steiner, Jürg, *Amicable Agreement versus Majority Rule: Conflict Resolution in Switzerland,* Chapel Hill, 1974.

3. The Anglo-American Countries

A. General Works

Alford, Robert R., *Party and Society: The Anglo-American Democracies,* Chicago, 1963.

Carthy, Mary Peter, *Catholicism in English-speaking Countries,* London, 1964.

Sheed, F. J., *The Church and I,* London, 1974. (Memoirs of a veteran Catholic publicist who worked in Australia, England and the United States.)

B. Australia

Aitkin, Don, *Stability and Change in Australian Politics,* New York, 1977.

Albinski, Henry S., *Canadian and Australian Politics in Comparative Perspective,* New York, 1973.

Brennan, Niall, *The Politics of Catholics,* Melbourne, 1972.

Grattan, C. Hartley, *The Southwest Pacific to 1900,* Ann Arbor, 1963.

Irvine, William P., and H. Gold, 'Do frozen cleavages ever go stale? The bases of the Canadian and Australian party systems', *British Journal of Political Science,* 10/2 (April 1980), 187–218.

Kemp, D. A., *Society and Electoral Behaviour in Australia: a Study of Three Decades,* St. Lucia, Qld., 1978.

Loveday, P., and A. W. Martin, *Parliament, Factions and Parties: the First Thirty Years of Responsible Government in New South Wales, 1856–1889,* Melbourne, 1966.

Mayer, Henry (ed.), *Catholics and the Free Society: an Australian Symposium,* Melbourne, 1961.

Mol, Hans, 'Religion and political allegiance', *Australian Journal of Politics and History,* XVI/3 (Dec. 1970), 320–33.

Mol, Hans, *Religion in Australia: a Sociological Investigation*, Melbourne, 1971.

Molony, John N., *The Roman Mould of the Australian Catholic Church,* Melbourne, 1969.

Murray, Robert, *The Split: Australian Labor in the Fifties*, Melbourne, 1970.

Murtagh, James G., *Australia: the Catholic Chapter*, 2nd edn., Sydney, 1959.

O'Farrell, Patrick, *The Catholic Church in Australia: a Short History, 1788–1967*, Melbourne, 1968.

O'Farrell, Patrick, *The Catholic Church and Community in Australia: a History*, Melbourne, 1977.

Ormonde, Paul, *The Movement*, Melbourne, 1972.

Rawson, D. W., *Australian Votes: the 1958 Federal Election*, Melbourne, 1961.

Reynolds, P. L., *The Democratic Labor Party*, Milton, Qld., 1974.

Truman, Tom, *Catholic Action and Politics*, 2nd edn., Melbourne, 1960.

C. Canada

Albinski, Henry S. – see under Australia.

Anderson, Grace M., 'Voting behaviour and the ethnic-religious variable: a study of a federal election in Hamilton, Ontario', *Canadian Journal of Economics and Political Science*, XXXII/1 (Feb. 1966), 27–37.

Ballantyne, Murray G., 'The Catholic Church and the C.C.F.', *Canadian Catholic Historical Association: Report 1963*, 33–45.

Beck, J. Murray, *Pendulum of Power: Canada's Federal Elections*, Scarborough, Ont., 1968.

Bernard, Jean-Paul, *Les rouges: libéralisme, nationalisme et anti-cléricalisme au milieu du XIXe siècle*, Montreal, 1971.

Blishen, B. R. *et al.* (eds.), *Canadian Society*, 3rd edn., New York, 1968.

Careless, J. M. S., *The Union of the Canadas: the Growth of Canadian Institutions, 1841–1857*, Toronto, 1967.

Chabot, Richard, *Le curé de campagne et la contestation locale au Québec (de 1791 aux troubles de 1837–38)*, Montreal, 1975.

Cornell, Paul G., *The Alignment of Political Groups in Canada 1841–1867*, Toronto, 1962.

Crysdale, Stewart, and Les Wheatcroft (eds.), *Religion in Canadian Society*, Toronto, 1976.

Dion, Gérard, 'Secularisation in Quebec', *Journal of Canadian Studies*, II, (1968), 35–44.

Dupont, Antonin, 'Louis-Alexandre Taschereau et la législation sociale au Québec, 1920–1936', *Revue d'Histoire de l'Amérique française*, 26/3 (Dec. 1972), 397–426.

Garner, John, *The Franchise and Politics in British North America, 1755–1867*, Toronto, 1969.

Grant, John Webster, *The Church in the Canadian Era*, Toronto, 1972. *A History of the Christian Church in Canada*, Vol. 3.

Gunn, Gertrude E., *The Political History of Newfoundland 1832–1864*, Toronto, 1966.

Hamelin, Jean et Marcel, *Les moeurs électorales dans le Québec de 1791 à nos jours*, Montreal, 1962.

Handy, Robert T., *A History of the Churches in the United States and Canada*, Oxford, 1976.

Hulliger, Jean, *L'enseignement social des évêques canadiens de 1891 à 1950*, Montreal, 1958.

Hurtubise, Pierre, *et al.*, *Le laic dans l'Eglise canadienne-française de 1830 à nos jours*, Montreal, 1972.

Irvine, William P., 'Explaining the religious basis of the Canadian partisan identity: success on the third try', *Canadian Journal of Political Science*, VII/3 (Sept. 1974), 560–3.

Irvine, William P., and H. Gold – see under Australia.

Le Blanc, Philip, and Arnold Edinborough (eds.), *One Church, Two Nations?* Don Mills, Ontario, 1968.

Meisel, John, *Working Papers on Canadian Politics*, 2nd edn., Montreal, 1973.

Moir, John S., *Church and State in Canada in Canada West*, Toronto, 1959.

Moir, John S., *The Church in the British Era*, Toronto, 1972. *A History of the Christian Church in Canada*, Vol. 2.

Moreux, Colette, *Fin d'une religion? Monographie d'une paroisse canadienne-française*, Montreal, 1969.

Morton, W. L., *The Critical Years: the Union of British North America, 1857–73*, Toronto, 1964.

Moulton, E. C., 'Constitutional crisis and civil strife in Newfoundland, February to November 1861', *Canadian Historical Review*, XLVIII/3 (Sept. 1967), 251–72.

Noel, S. J. R., *Politics in Newfoundland*, Toronto, 1971.

Norman, E. R., *The Conscience of the State in North America*, Cambridge, England, 1968.

Ouellet, Fernand, *Le Bas Canada 1791–1840: changements structuraux et crise*, Ottawa, 1976.

Plante, Hermann, *L'Eglise catholique au Canada (1604–1886)*, Trois-Rivières, 1970.

Porter, John, *The Vertical Mosaic: an Analysis of Social Class and Power in Canada*, Toronto, 1975.

Quinn, Herbert, F., *The Union Nationale: a Study in Quebec Nationalism*, Toronto, 1963.

Robin, Martin (ed.), *Canadian Provincial Politics*, Scarborough, Ont., 1972.

Voisine, Nive, *et al., Histoire de l'Eglise catholique au Québec (1608–1970)*, Montreal, 1971.

Wade, Mason, *The French Canadians*, 2 vols., 2nd edn., New York, 1968.

Waite, Peter B., *Canada, 1874–1896*, Toronto, 1971.

Watt, James T., 'Anti-Catholic nativism in Canada: the Protestant Protective Association', *Canadian Historical Review*, XLVIII/1 (Mar. 1967), 45–58.

Westhues, Kenneth, 'Nationalisme et catholicisme canadien', *Concilium* (Paris), 131 (Jan. 1978), 61–8.

Woodrow, Alain, 'Le Québec: "tranquillement, très vite"', *Informations Catholiques internationales*, 410/15 (June 1972), 9–16.

D. Ireland

Works on Northern Ireland are included under the United Kingdom.

Akenson, Donald H., *The Irish Education Experiment*, London, 1970.

Akenson, Donald H., *A Mirror to Kathleen's Face: Education in Independent Ireland 1922–1960*, Montreal, 1975.

Bowen, Desmond, *The Protestant Crusade in Ireland 1800–70*, Dublin, 1978.

Broderick, John F., *The Holy See and the Irish Movement for the Repeal of the Union with England, 1829–1847*, Rome, 1951.

Corish, Patrick J., 'Political problems, 1860–78', in P. J. Corish (ed.), *A History of Irish Catholicism*, vol. 5, fascicule 2/3, Dublin, 1967.

Jupp, P. J., 'Irish parliamentary elections and the influence of the Catholic vote, 1801–20', *Historical Journal*, X/2 (1967), 183–96.

Larkin, Emmet, *The Historical Dimensions of Irish Catholicism*, New York, 1976.

Larkin, Emmet, 'Launching the counterattack: the Roman Catholic hierarchy and the destruction of Parnellism', *Review of Politics*, 25 (1963), 152–182 and 28 (1966), 359–83.

Larkin, Emmet, *The Roman Catholic Church and the Creation of the Modern Irish State 1878–1886*, Dublin, 1975.

Larkin, Emmet, 'Socialism and Catholicism in Ireland', *Church History*, XXXIII (Dec. 1964), 462–83.

Lyons, F. S. L., *John Dillon*, London, 1968.

MacDonagh, Oliver, 'The politicization of the Irish Catholic bishops, 1800–1850', *Historical Journal*, XVIII/1 (1975), 37–53.

Miller, David W., *Church, State and Nation in Ireland, 1898–1921*, Dublin, 1973.

Norman, E. R., *The Catholic Church and Ireland in the Age of Rebellion, 1859–1873*, London, 1965.

O'Farrell, Patrick, *Ireland's English Question*, London, 1971.
Tierney, Mark, *Croke of Cashel*, Dublin, 1976.
Whyte, J. H., *Church and State in Modern Ireland, 1923–1979*, 2nd edn., Dublin, 1980.
Whyte, J. H., 'Church, State and Society, 1950–70', in J. J. Lee (ed.), *Ireland 1945–70*, Dublin, 1979, 73–82.
Whyte, J. H., *The Independent Irish Party, 1850–9*, Oxford, 1958.
Whyte, J. H., 'The influence of the Catholic clergy on elections in nineteenth-century Ireland', *English Historical Review*, LXXV/195, (April 1960), 239–59.
Whyte, J. H., '1916 – Revolution and religion', in F. X. Martin (ed.), *Leaders and Men of the Easter Rising: Dublin 1916*, London, 1966, 215–26.
Whyte, J. H., 'Political problems, 1850–60', in P. J. Corish (ed.), *A History of Irish Catholicism*, vol. 5, fascicule 2/3, Dublin, 1967.

E. New Zealand

Chapman, R. M., W. K. Jackson and A. V. Mitchell, *New Zealand Politics in Action: the 1960 General Election*, London, 1962.
Davis, R. P., 'The New Zealand Labour Party's "Irish campaign", 1916–1921', *Political Science*, 19/2 (1967), 13–23.
Davis, R. P., 'Sir George Grey and Irish Nationalism', *New Zealand Journal of History*, 1/2 (Oct. 1967)), 185–98.
Grattan, C. Hartley – see under Australia.
Laracy, Hugh, 'Paranoid popery: Bishop Moran and Catholic education in New Zealand', *New Zealand Journal of History*, 10 (1976), 51–62.
Lipson, Leslie, *The Politics of Equality: New Zealand's Adventures in Democracy*, Chicago, 1948.
Mackey, John, *The Making of a State Education System: the Passing of the New Zealand Education Act, 1877*, London, 1967.
Milne, R. S., *Political Parties in New Zealand*, Oxford, 1966.
Milne, R. S., 'Voting in Wellington Central, 1957', *Political Science*, 10/2 (Sept. 1958), 31–64.
Mitchell, Austin, *Politics and People in New Zealand*, Christchurch, 1969.
O'Connor, P. S., 'Sectarian conflict in New Zealand, 1911–1920', *Political Science*, 19 (July 1967), 3–16.
O'Farrell, P. J., *Harry Holland, Militant Socialist*, Canberra, 1964.

F. United Kingdom

A number of the titles listed under Ireland are also relevant to the United Kingdom.

Bealey, Frank, J. Blondel and W. P. McCann, *Constituency Politics: a Study of Newcastle-under Lyme*, London, 1965.
Beck, G. A. (ed.), *The English Catholics, 1850–1950*, London, 1950.
Benney, Mark, A. P. Gray and R. H. Pear, *How People Vote: a Study of Electoral Behaviour in Greenwich*, London, 1956.
Blewett, Neal, *The Peers, the Parties and the People: the General Elections of 1910*, London, 1972.
Brand, Sister M. Vivian, *The Social Catholic Movement in England, 1920–1955*, New York, 1963.
Butler, David, and Donald Stokes, *Political Change in Britain: the Evolution of Electoral Choice*, 2nd edn., London, 1974.
Catholicisme anglais, Paris, 1958.
Chadwick, Owen, *The Victorian Church*, 2 vols., 2nd edn., London, 1971–2.
Clarke, P. F., *Lancashire and the New Liberalism*, Cambridge, 1971.
Cleary, J. M., *Catholic Social Action in Britain, 1909–1959*, Oxford, 1961.
Coman, Peter, *Catholics and the Welfare State*, London, 1977.
Currie, Robert, Alan Gilbert and Lee Horsley, *Churches and Churchgoers: Patterns of Church Growth in the British Isles since 1700*, Oxford, 1977.
Handley, James, E., *The Irish in Modern Scotland*, Cork, 1947.
Handley, James E., *The Irish in Scotland, 1798–1845*, Cork, 1943.
Hanham, H. J., *Elections and Party Management: Politics in the Time of Disraeli and Gladstone*, London, 1959.
Highet, John, *The Scottish Churches*, London, 1960.
Hoppen, K. T., 'Tories, Catholics, and the general election of 1859', *Historical Journal*, XIII/1 (1970), 48–67.
Howard, C. H. D., 'The Parnell manifesto of 21 November 1885, and the schools question', *English Historical Review*, LXII/242 (Jan. 1947), 42–51.
Jackson, John A., *The Irish in Britain*, London, 1963.
McCaffrey, John, 'The Irish vote in Glasgow in the later nineteenth century: a preliminary survey', *Innes Review*, XXI/1 (Spring 1970), 30–36.
McClelland, Vincent Alan, *Cardinal Manning: His Public Life and Influence, 1865–1892*, London, 1962.
MacEntee, Georgina Putnam, *The Social Catholic Movement in Great Britain*, New York, 1927.
Machin, G. I. T., *The Catholic Question in English Politics, 1820 to 1830*, Oxford, 1964.
Machin, G. I. T., *Politics and the Churches in Great Britain, 1832 to 1868*, Oxford, 1977.
Martin, Bernice, 'Comments on some Gallup poll statistics', in

David Martin (ed.), *A Sociological Yearbook of Religion in Britain,* London, 1968.

Martin, David, *A Sociology of English Religion,* London, 1967.

Mayor, Stephen, *The Churches and the Labour Movement,* London, 1967.

Middleton, Neil, *et al., 'Slant Manifesto': Catholics and the Left,* London, 1966.

Murphy, James, *Church, State and Schools in Britain, 1800–1970,* London, 1971.

Norman, E. R., *Anti-Catholicism in Victorian England,* London, 1968.

Pelling, Henry, *Social Geography of British Elections, 1885–1910,* London, 1967.

Pulzer, Peter J. G., *Political Representation and Elections in Britain,* 3rd edn., London, 1975.

Rose, Richard, *Governing without consensus: an Irish Perspective,* London, 1971. (On Northern Ireland.)

Scott, George, *The R.C.s: a Report on Roman Catholics in Britain Today,* London, 1967.

The Times, 17 April 1975. Letter from Hugh Lindsay, Bishop of Hexham and Newcastle, providing church-attendance figures.

Vincent, John, *The Formation of the British Liberal Party,* London, 1966.

Vincent, J. R., *Pollbooks: How Victorians Voted,* Cambridge, England, 1967.

Walker, W. M., 'Irish immigrants in Scotland: their priests, politics and parochial life', *Historical Journal,* XV/4 (1972), 649–67.

G. United States

Abell, Aaron I., *American Catholicism and Social Action: a Search for Social Justice, 1865–1950,* Garden City, N.Y., 1960.

Abramson, Harold J., *Ethnic Diversity in Catholic America,* New York, 1973.

Adams, James L., *The Growing Church Lobby in Washington,* Grand Rapids, 1970.

Alston, John P., 'Social variables associated with church attendance, 1965 and 1969: evidence from national polls', *Journal for the Scientific Study of Religion,* 10/3 (Fall 1971), 233–6.

Axelrod, Robert, 'Where the votes come from: an analysis of electoral coalitions, 1952–1968', *American Political Science Review,* LXVI/1 (Mar. 1972), 11–20.

Billington, Ray Allen, *The Protestant Crusade, 1800–1860,* New York, 1938.

Broderick, Francis L., *Right Reverend New Dealer: John A. Ryan,* New York, 1963.

Brown, Thomas N., *Irish-American Nationalism, 1870–1890,* Philadelphia, 1966.

Buetow, Harold A., *Of Singular Benefit: the Story of Catholic Education in the United States,* New York, 1970.

Burnham, Walter Dean – see under Germany.

Callahan, Daniel, 'Contraception and abortion: American Catholic responses', *Annals of the American Academy of Political Science,* 38 (Jan. 1970), 109–17.

Campbell, Angus, Philip E. Converse, Warren E. Miller and Donald E. Stokes, *Elections and the Political Order,* New York, 1967.

Clark, Dennis, *The Irish in Philadelphia: Ten Generations of Urban Experience,* Philadelphia, 1973.

Cosman, Bernard, 'Religion and race in Louisiana presidential politics, 1960', *Southwestern Social Science Quarterly,* 43/3 (Dec. 1962), 235–41.

Cross, Robert D., *The Emergence of Liberal Catholicism in America,* Cambridge, Mass., 1958.

Curry, Lerond, *Protestant-Catholic Relations in America: World War I through Vatican II,* Lexington, Ky., 1972.

Dienes, C. Thomas, *Law, Politics, and Birth Control,* Urbana, 1972.

Ellis, John Tracy, *American Catholicism,* 2nd edn., Chicago, 1969.

Ellis, John Tracy (ed.), *The Catholic Priest in the United States: Historical Investigations,* Collegeville, Minn., 1971.

Fenton, John H., *The Catholic Vote,* New Orleans, 1960.

Fenton, John H., *Midwest Politics,* New York, 1966.

Fischer, David Hackett, *The Revolution of American Conservatism,* New York, 1965.

Foner, Philip S., *History of the Labour Movement in the United States, III: the Policies and Practices of the American Federation of Labour, 1900–1909,* New York, 1964.

Fuchs, Lawrence H. (ed.), *American Ethnic Politics,* New York, 1968.

Fuchs, Lawrence H., *John F. Kennedy and American Catholicism,* New York, 1967.

Gleason, Philip, *The Conservative Reformers: German-American Catholics and the Social Order,* Notre Dame, 1968.

Gleason, Philip (ed.), *Contemporary Catholicism in the United States,* Notre Dame, 1969.

Glock, Charles Y., and Rodney Stark, *Religion and Society in Tension,* Chicago, 1965.

Greeley, Andrew M., William C. McCready and Kathleen McCourt, *Catholic Schools in a Declining Church,* Kansas City, 1976.

Greeley, Andrew M. and Peter H. Rossi, *The Education of Catholic Americans,* Chicago, 1966.

Handy, Robert T. – see under Canada.

Hanna, Mary T., *Catholics and American Politics,* Cambridge, Mass., 1979.

Herberg, Will, *Protestant–Catholic–Jew,* 2nd edn., Garden City, N.Y., 1960.

Higham, John, *Strangers in the Land: Patterns of American Nativism 1860–1925,* 2nd edn., New York, 1963.

Houtart, François, *Aspects sociologiques du catholicisme américain,* Paris, 1957.

Howard, Perry H., *Political Tendencies in Louisiana,* 2nd edn., Baton Rouge, 1971.

Kane, John J., *Catholic-Protestant Conflicts in America,* Chicago, 1955.

Kleppner, Paul, *The Cross of Culture: a Social Analysis of Midwestern Politics 1850–1900,* New York, 1970.

Knoke, David, *Change and Continuity in American Politics: the Social Bases of Political Parties,* Baltimore, 1976.

Knoke, David, 'Religion, stratification and politics: America in the 1960s', *American Journal of Political Science,* 18/2 (May 1974), 331–45.

Ladd, Everett Carll, Jr., with Charles D. Hadley, *Transformations of the American Party System,* New York, 1975.

Lannie, Vincent P., *Public Money and Parochial Education: Bishop Hughes, Governor Seward, and the New York School Controversy,* Cleveland, 1968

Lapomarda, Vincent A., 'A Jesuit runs for Congress: the Rev. Robert F. Drinan, S.J., and his 1970 campaign', *Journal of Church and State,* 15/2 (Spring 1973), 205–22.

Laslett, John H. M., and S. M. Lipset (eds.), *Failure of a Dream? Essays in the History of American Socialism,* Garden City, N.Y., 1974.

Lazerwitz, Bernard, 'Religion and social structure in the United States', in Louis Schneider (ed.), *Religion, Culture and Society,* New York, 1964, 426–39.

Lenski, Gerhard, *The Religious Factor,* 2nd edn., Garden City, N.Y., 1963.

Lipset, S. M., 'Religion and politics in the American past and present', in Robert Lee and Martin Marty (eds.), *Religion and Social Conflict,* New York, 1964, 69–112. Also in S. M. Lipset, *Revolution and Counter-revolution,* New York, 1968, 246–303.

Lockard, Duane, *New England State Politics,* Princeton, 1959.

McAvoy, Thomas T., *The Great Crisis in American Catholic History, 1895–1900,* Notre Dame, 1963.

McAvoy, Thomas T., *A History of the Catholic Church in the United States,* Notre Dame, 1969.

McSeveney, Samuel T., *The Politics of Depression: Political Behavior in the Northeast, 1893–1896,* New York, 1972.

Marcus, Sheldon, *Father Coughlin,* Boston, 1973.

Morgan, Richard E., *The Politics of Religious Conflict,* New York, 1968.

Nie, Norman H., Sidney Verba and John R. Petrocik, *The Changing American Voter,* Cambridge, Mass., 1976.

Norman, E. R. – see under Canada.

Potter, David M., *The Impending Crisis, 1848–1861,* New York, 1976.

Putz, Louis J. (ed.), *The Catholic Church, U.S.A.,* Chicago, 1956.

Raab, Earl (ed.), *Religious Conflict in America,* Garden City, N.Y., 1964.

Schlesinger, Arthur M., Jr. (ed.), *History of U.S. Political Parties,* 4 vols., New York, 1973.

Silbey, Joel H., Allan G. Bogue and William H. Flanigan (eds.), *The History of American Electoral Behavior,* Princeton, 1978.

Stedman, Murray S., Jr., *Religion and Politics in America,* New York, 1964.

Tavard, George H., *Catholicism U.S.A.,* New York, 1969.

Underwood, Kenneth W., *Protestant and Catholic,* Boston, 1957.

4. Malta

Austin, Dennis, *Malta and the End of Empire,* London, 1971.

Boissevain, Jeremy, *Saints and Fireworks,* London, 1965.

Dobie, Edith, *Malta's Road to Independence,* Norman, Okla., 1967.

Index